THE KINGS OF SLATE CREEK

LARRY LIVENGOOD

ISBN: 979-8218084110 (Hardcover)
ISBN: 979-8218085230 (Paperback)

Library of Congress Control Number: 2022918424

Second Edition

Published by Alexandra Runyon

In memory of my wife,

Juanita Livengood.

Table of Contents

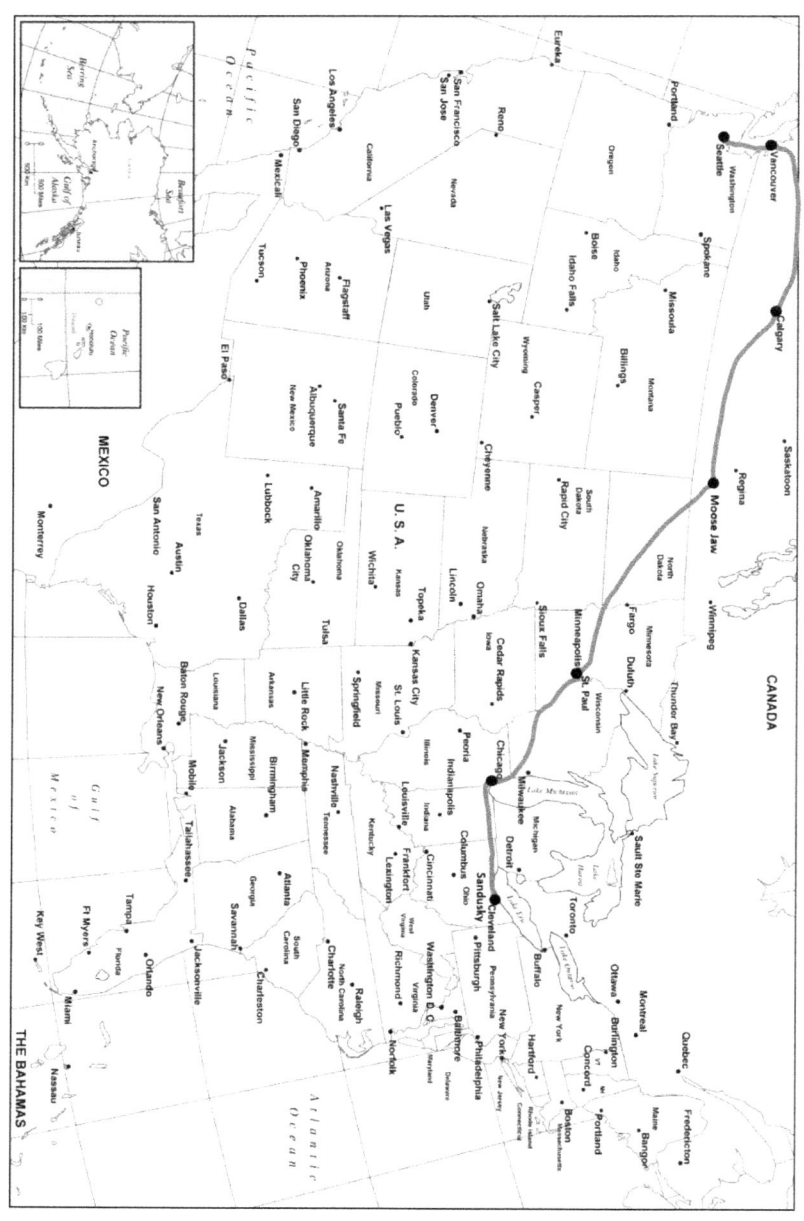

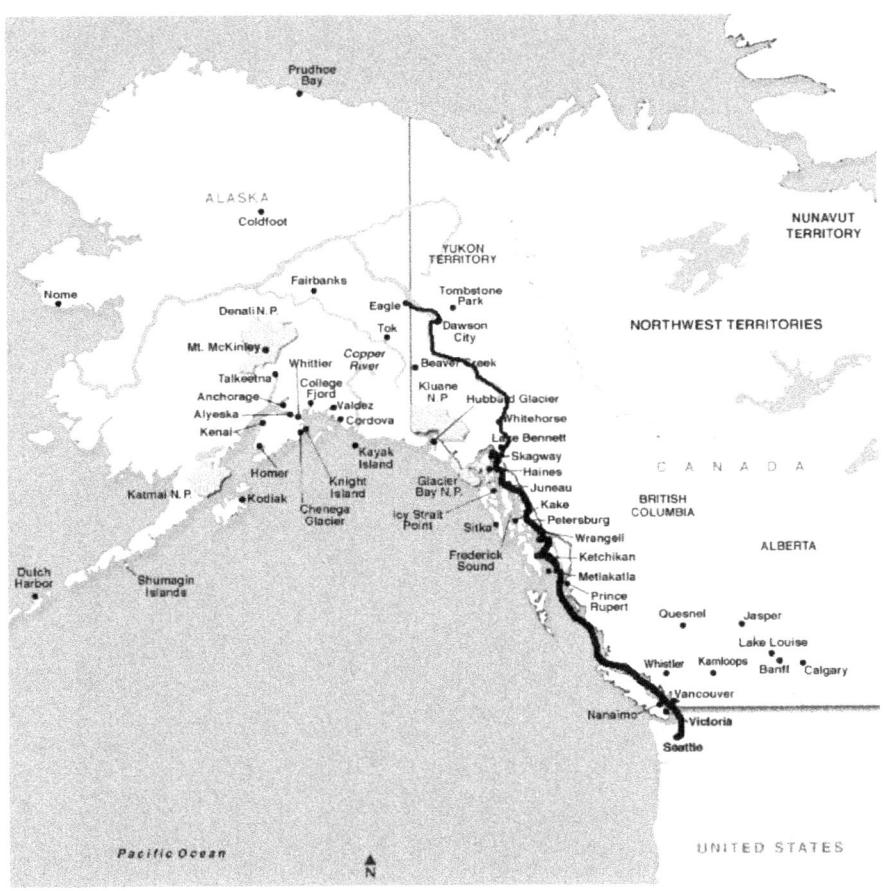

Remember the year of the Big Stampede and the trail of Ninety-eight,

When the eyes of the world were turned to the North, and the hearts of men elate:

Hearts of the old dare-devil breed thrilled at the wonderous strike,

And to every man who could hold a pan came the message, "Up and hike."

Well, I was there with the best of them, and I knew I would not fail.

You wouldn't believe it to see me now; but wait till you've heard my tale.

Robert Service

Preface

In 1897, my grandfather, Ross Livengood, and his first cousin, Jay Livengood, were chosen by the directors of a newly formed mining co-operative to join a group of men that they were sending to the Klondike region of Canada to prospect for gold. The company, headquartered in Sandusky, Ohio, was organized by five local businessmen who agreed to direct and invest in the venture. The company's goal was to profit from the recent gold discoveries in Canada that were being chronicled in newspapers across the nation.

The ensuing saga of the "Sandusky Klondikers," as they were called is based upon letters that the prospectors sent home to their friends and families. The letters, which were reprinted in the local newspapers, related details of their daily activities as they searched for gold in the wilderness of Alaska.

All the participants signed a contract binding them in a cooperative effort to search for gold and stake their claims in the Klondike region of Canada. The duration of the contract was set to be 18 months, after which they would return to Sandusky. The anticipated profits from the sale of the gold and mining claims were to be divided, with half going to the investors and the other half to be split proportionately among the miners.

The Klondikers' expedition was flexible and well planned. The contract allowed for operational changes to be made by an advisory committee if new information, or unforeseen circumstances, warranted it. The plan called for the men to haul their goods from Sandusky to Seattle by rail before continuing from Seattle to Skagway, Alaska by ship. Upon arrival at Skagway, everything they would need to sustain themselves would have to be carried up and over the White Pass trail to Lake Bennett. While camping that winter at Lake Bennett they would build boats to float their supplies down the Yukon River to the gold fields near Dawson in the Yukon Territory. Once the ice broke up on the Yukon River in the spring of 1898, the six-hundred-mile voyage would begin.

The men set out in high spirits in anticipation of the adventure and challenges of the trail. Their endeavor went smoothly until they reached Dawson, where they were greeted by unexpected and dire circumstances. Upon arrival they soon encountered the Royal Canadian Mounted Police who were there to enforce Canada's strict mining rules and high taxes. They found that the rich claims that had been reported in the newspapers had all been taken, and like thousands of others they had arrived too late. The town was in near chaos. Food and supplies were becoming scarce due to ice blocking the supply boats on the Yukon River. The people of Dawson were beginning to panic.

Frustrated by the conditions in Dawson, the Sandusky party decided to sail ten miles farther down the Yukon River into Alaskan territory and set up their headquarters at Eagle City.

When the company arrived in Eagle, they readily obtained several building sites and selected a team to build their warehouse and cabin before winter set in. While some of the men stayed behind to continue building the warehouse, other teams set out to explore and prospect the surrounding creeks for gold. Some of the creeks they scoured were as far as forty miles away from their headquarters at Eagle. A dozen or more mining claims were established in various creeks in the area that summer.

If the camp's provisions were in ample supply, the men worked diligently, and morale was high. However, by the end of the summer of 1898 their supplies and funds began to run low. The men's tools and clothing were quickly wearing out. Scurvy and injuries crippled some of the men, and for the first time a spirit of dejection and gloom fell over the camp. Suspicions of theft, and whispered rumors of deceit by their captain, began to undermine the men's confidence in his leadership. After a chaotic confrontation, accusations and charges of theft were made against him, and the men demanded that a miners-court trial be held. The trial resulted in the expulsion of their leader from Alaska as dictated by miners' law, which was the only law in the land at the time.

A new leader was chosen by the men, funds and supplies eventually arrived from Sandusky, and the camp settled down and returned to normal. Unfortunately, their trials were not over. The following spring, when the ice broke up once again on the rivers, a massive flood washed out the dam. The dam had been built on Slate Creek to protect their most promising claim. Water flooded the mine. It was too late to start over. The past winter's work on the Slate Creek mine had all been washed away.

Come June, the duration of the contract was complete. The quest ended for most of the party when they boarded a river boat for their return to Ohio. Two company representatives stayed in Eagle to sell out the claims and buildings, but a few, including Ross and Jay who would not admit defeat, chose to stay in Alaska and join the new stampede to Nome. They would now be on their own.

Although the adventure was deemed by some to have been a bust, in 1958 when Ross was asked by a news reporter if he had brought back any gold he declared, "Well, I didn't come home rich but then I didn't come home C.O.D. either. All in all, I wouldn't have missed it for the world".[1]

Ross and Larry Livengood- 1938

---

[1] "Milan Farmer Recalls", *Sandusky Register,* 5 July 1958

-1898-

THE KINGS OF SLATE CREEK

The story of the Sandusky Klondikers is told by the adventurers themselves and described in their own words in their letters from the Klondike.

Sandusky, Ohio

1897, history books called them "The Gay Nineties" when describing life in America during the 1890's. But "gay" would hardly describe life in rural America where a dreary depression brought on by exceedingly low farm prices gripped the countryside. The economy of Erie County, which is located along the southern shores of Lake Erie, was highly influenced by agriculture. Progress or change came at a very slow pace for the people living on the farms or in the small, rural crossroad towns, such as Flat Rock, Parkertown, and Enterprise located to the south of Sandusky.

At Sand Hill Rosannah Livengood helped support her family by renting out rooms and taking in boarders. Rosanna's husband Seth had died of typhus in1879. Rose and her sons Seth jr. and Jay, along with the boarders made up the household while Rose's oldest son David lived next door, where he operated a blacksmith shop. Jay was employed as a stonecutter at a nearby limestone quarry.

In later years Seth jr. related, "We would never have made it through those hard times if our Uncle Urban hadn't helped us out with produce from his farm at Enterprise."[2] Urban was an elder brother of their late father, Seth, who looked out for Rose's family after her husband's death. Despite these dreary times, events that were occurring on Americas west coast were about to have a stunning effect on the lives of Rosanna's family.

---

[2] Interview with Seth Livengood by Helen Livengood, the author's mother, in the 1940's

On July 19, 1897, the *Excelsior*, a passenger ship nine days out of St. Michaels, Alaska arrived in port at San Francisco. Gaunt, mud-spattered miners lined the deck rails. Their clothes and baggage were worn and tattered but filled with gold. At that moment, the stampede for gold in the Klondike began. Not quietly or gradually, but instantaneously and with explosive force. Two days later, when a second ship arrived at Seattle with its decks also piled with bags of gold, a mass lunacy seized the nation. It is said that one million people made plans to go to the Klondike, but only one hundred thousand did set off to make the trip. Having endured those drab depression years, the fantasy of easy riches compelled many to desert their jobs and families to chase a 'will-o-wisp' in an uncharted land far to the north. It requires time for such a massive army of men and equipment to get under way and it was already late in July. Alaska starts to freeze up by September so the mass movement wouldn't begin until the following spring.[3]

At first the news of a gold strike in the Klondike and the ensuing stampede held only a passing interest to the people living in Erie County. It wasn't until *The Sandusky Daily Register* headlines announced "THEY'RE GOING TO ALASKA" that local interest was aroused. The story described a plan by several Sandusky merchants and a prominent banker to form a co-operative gold mining company to go to Alaska and attempt to bring back a fortune in gold. The announcement of the speculative plan brought home to Sandusky the excitement of a gold strike in far off Alaska and immediately changed it from national headlines to a local story.

---

[3] Pierre Burton, The Klondike Quest, *Boston Mills Press,* 1983, 1997

The company planned to sponsor a score or more of Sandusky's young and middle-aged men, some of them prominent in business and society, to leave in early spring. The company was to be capitalized by selling $20,000 worth of stock at $10 a share. No one was to hold more than 25 shares of stock.

October 19, 1897, newspapers announced that a meeting for those interested in the Alaskan adventure would be held in Mahala hall the following evening at 7:30, and the public cordially invited to attend. An interesting lecture on Alaska and her great gold fields was to be delivered by Mr. J.E. Snevely, who had spent two and a half years in that land. The speaker had a large map of the country and an enticing speech prepared. The purpose of the meeting was to push the organization of the proposed company. It was said that there were so many ready to take stock that some would have to be refused.[4]

Urban Livengood's youngest son Ross attended the meeting that night with Jay as a large crowd filled Mahala hall. As plans for the venture were laid out to the public the boy's interest grew, and they were soon quite excited about having an opportunity to take part in such an adventure. After the meeting a note pad was passed around for those who were interested in joining the company to list their names. It was no surprise that the number of adventurers willing to sign on for the venture far exceeded the twenty men proposed by the planners. There appeared to be no shortage of willing participants.

---

[4] They're Going to Alaska, *Sandusky Daily Register,* 19 October 1897

On December 20, 1897, a *Sandusky Daily Register* story related that an enthusiastic meeting was held the past Saturday night at the Slone House, and the newly formed Alaska Co-operative Mining Company was organized and incorporated. The purpose of the corporation was to grubstake 20 participants who were willing to invest in 30 shares of stock each and go to the North land under a contract. The rules of the contract were settled upon such that the men would operate in a co-operative manner, and the majority would always rule. Half of what they found would go to the company, and the other half was to be divided proportionately among the participants. Of those who went, none were expected to return before September of 1899, and some would never come back at all. The directors of the company were decided to be C. L. Warner, A. E. Merrill[5], J.C. Scheufler, F.L. Felch, and J.C. Parsons, all of whom were prominent businessmen of Sandusky.

The Norwalk members of the party brought their attorney to the meeting to examine the contract. A physician was called to examine the physical fitness of 14 of the young men. Upon being confirmed to be perfectly sound and physically able to withstand the rigors of the long journey, it was announced that the company would be leaving Sandusky on February 1st, with a complete outfit and provisions enough to last them for 18 months. J.E. Snevely, who had much experience in Alaska, would pilot the party as a general manager and mining engineer. The party would have an assayer and outfit, an engineer with a commission as deputy United States Surveyor, and a notary public, so that it would essentially carry the law of the land along with it. The list of 23 included in the party was

---

[5] A. E. Merrill owned the *Sandusky Journal* Newspaper in 1897

reported, but it was also noted there might possibly be one or two last minute changes before departure.[6]

The list of participants was changing almost daily as some of the men reconsidered and withdrew their names for one reason or another, with others moving up on the list taking the former's places. Coincidently, two of the men who made this early list are related to Jay's future wife, Olive Doerflinger. Charles Koegle, who was Olive's uncle, as well as her brother Frank, had also made the list. Frank would later withdraw from the group as did quite a few of the others before the final roll was settled upon.

A significant addition to the list of miners was that of Howard Huntington. Howard, the son of a prominent Sandusky businessman and a Harvard graduate, was also to be a special correspondent for the *New York Post* newspaper. Howard had agreed to post stories relating the miner's experiences as they traveled to the goldfields. Because of his educational background he was also appointed secretary to the Captain, J.E. Snevely. By February, cousins Jay and Ross Livengood had made the list.

Ross was later quoted as saying, "I made the list on the day before the company was scheduled to leave. There was a Milan butcher who got cold feet and pulled out, so I jumped at the chance to take his place."[7]

The Saturday edition of *The Sandusky Daily Register* announced that on the following Monday evening at 5:33 o'clock, the Lake Shore west bound train pulled out of Sandusky carrying the 20 young men and their provisions on a journey clear through to

---

[6] Pulls Out in Six Weeks, *Sandusky Daily Register,* 20 December 1897
[7] Milan Farmer Recalls, *Sandusky Register,* 5 July 1958

Seattle, on the west coast. They had an outfit weighing about 25 tons. Among the hundreds of items were 8000 pounds of flour, 2000 pounds of hard bread, 2000 pounds of white corn, 3000 pounds of navy beans, and 3000 pounds of sugar-cured bacon. A representative of the Lake Shore railway accompanied the party to Chicago, then another from there to St. Paul and still another thence to Seattle. The party arrived in Chicago Tuesday morning and remained until evening to make their final purchases. At Seattle, a stop of a week was be made before passage was taken on some northbound ship, and during that time it was be determined what route would be taken. A Register correspondent would accompany the party, and its readers would be kept posted on the Klondikers' movements and discoveries. Interesting letters from the party to their many friends at home would be published regularly.[8]

On Monday, February 7, the long-awaited day of departure for the Sandusky party of miners finally arrived. The morning was cold with a wind blowing in from the north sending low scudding clouds across the Sandusky Bay and bringing with it a mixture of snow and sleet- a harbinger of the cold days of adventure that lay ahead. After noon the sun appeared briefly, and the day warmed slightly. About 2:00 o'clock, an hour before train time, a crowd began to gather at the Lake Shore depot. They arrived on foot, in buggies by streetcar, and any way they could, and when the west bound train came rolling in, the wondering passengers gazed out of their windows upon a noisy throng of 3,000, crowding each other from one end of the platform to the other.

---

[8] Gold of the Klondike, *Sandusky Daily Register,* 5 February 1898

Suddenly a mighty cheer went up from the crowd of onlookers. This was the signal that proclaimed the coming of the special car set aside especially for the Sandusky party. It was a pretty coach, new and brilliantly polished. The coach was coupled to the rear of the train, and one by one the Klondikers stepped aboard while their baggage was being taken on the express car. As the bell on the locomotive began to ring the crowd became excited. They tried to reach into the coach and shake hands one last time with those on board—for all were now inside with the windows raised. Puff, Puff, Puff! The train started. Three thousand men, woman, boys and girls yelled themselves hoarse. Hats were tossed and waved on high as people held the children up to see it all. Some Klondikers stood on the platform and smiled and bowed, while others hung out of the windows and shook hands with those along the line. The train went faster. The last person seen on it was Dell Deyo, waving his cap from the rear platform, while the wind whistled through his red whiskers. Soon only the red and green lights at the rear of the coach gleamed, and then disappeared, the noise of the puffing engine died away and it was all over. The train was gone. The crowd dispersed.

The party is as follows, with a few changes being made since the list was first published in the Register Saturday morning. J.E. Snevely, Dell J. Deyo, Wm. Fettle, A.H. Meinzer, Charles W. Koegle, Charles Smith, Howard C. Huntington, W.M. Thiem, Patrick H. McCrystal, George Miller and James Sanderson, of Sandusky; W.M. Cowan, F. Adleman and H.N. Zurcher, Norwalk; Ross Livengood, Milan: J. Livengood, Sand Hill; George Gleckner, Lindsey; Perry Hutchins and J.L. Shay, Dayton; and Sylvester Widman, Kingsway.[9]

---

[9] Off for the Golden Land, *Sandusky Daily Register,* 9 February 1898

That morning Henry K. Henkelman, of the firm of Henkelman & Bechberger, local druggists, received a postal from Mr. Deyo himself, which ought to set at rest all fears, as it certainly gives the lie to the false and exaggerated rumors of gloom and doom. It is as follows[10]:

Castle Mountain[11],   Feb 12

Friend Henry:

I will send you a card from here as it is the most picturesque place we have seen. We are now passing through the mountains, and all are very much interested. It is a very warm, pleasant day and the sun is shining brightly. We have had a very pleasant trip so far. Remained in Chicago one day and in St. Paul 24 hours and are due in Seattle on Sunday evening. The boys are feeling first class and are enjoying their trip A-1, and if we have nothing worse than this will never come back to Sandusky. We have ridden many miles and without seeing a house of any kind. I will write you again from Seattle.

Yours, etc.

Dell Deyo

---

[10] The Klondike Party, *Norwalk Daily Reflector*, from the *Sandusky Journal*, 17 February 1898
[11] Castle Mountain, where the postal was mailed, is a station on the Canadian Pacific Road in the province of Alberta. It is about 10 hours' journey from Seattle, and about 1700 or 1800 miles from the city.

Seattle

The trip from Sandusky to Seattle was a pleasant journey taking seven days with twenty-four-hour stopovers at Chicago and Minneapolis. Upon arriving at Seattle, a storefront on 7th Street was leased to house their supplies while they waited to board ship. Since their plans were flexible at this juncture the leaders of the group sought out returning miners and people who were knowledgeable of the conditions that they would encounter in Alaska for advice on the best way to precede from there. Taking advantage of the best information available a decision was made to take the White Pass trail from Skaguay to Lake Bennett rather than the much steeper Chilkoot trail at Dyea. They purchased a pair of oxen enabling them to move their supplies by sled. Finally, the last of their supplies were purchased and passage was booked on the barque Theobald. The following letter was sent from Seattle.

Seattle Wash.   Feb.14, 1898

 Friend Harry:

    We arrived in this town last evening; and it is a lively one. Men here by the thousands, and all going to the gold fields, and everybody here is trying to get all the money that is possible to get. We will probably remain here for several days, and we may go at any time. It is warm here, but it is rainy and cloudy; but we have had very nice weather all the way, and the boys have been well and have enjoyed the trip immensely, and the sights cannot be described. Tell Mr. Gregory we came through all O.K. and did not have any trouble about showing any of our goods, and the atmosphere in Minnesota is grand. Henry, it is a fact that with the thermometer at two degrees below zero you do not feel it as bad as you do freezing in Sandusky. We got some mail this morning, but it is almost impossible to get to the office. There was a string of men reaching from your store down to the office. So you can imagine. One person is only allowed to get mail for two persons. My next will be from Alaska. Give my regards to all.

Yours Truly,

D.J. Deyo[12]

---

[12] From The Klondikers, *Norwalk Daily Reflector*, 21 February 1898

From the *Sandusky Register*

Sandusky's gold hunters, the party now bound Klondikeward, did not leave Seattle at the time previously announced, but are now on the broad bosom of the Pacific, having sailed Tuesday or Wednesday in the barque Theobold.

The following letter from Howard Huntington, private secretary to Manager Snevely, tells all about it.[13]

Seattle Wash.   Feb.27

Mr. J.C. Scheuffler, Secretary,

Sandusky, Ohio

Dear Sir:

At last we are through buying--- the outfit is complete---our passage engaged, and all is in readiness to go aboard the barque Theobold on Tuesday. We have delayed longer in Seattle than was at first intended, but the time has been pleasantly and profitably spent, and as all old Yukoners say the month of March is the best in which to cross the mountains by either Chilkoot or White pass we think we have done well in waiting for it.

In justice to Seattle merchants, we wish to say that the market here is just as well stocked and prices lower than we found them in Chicago and St. Paul. We were told in the east that prices were way up out here on the coast, but we find them very fair. The merchants

---

[13] Off For Klondike, Sandusky Daily Register, 28 Feb 1898

here know exactly the needs of the Alaskan miners and take pains to fill them at reasonable rates. We do not mean by eastern markets that of Sandusky, for by the home merchants we were very well treated, both in prices and in gifts. The calendar clock presented by Henry Dehnel keeps perfect time; the cigars from George Rinkleft, the cheese and crackers, gifts of Colonel Woodward, were thoroughly appreciated by all the boys on the trip to Seattle, while the chickens, dominoes and dictionary presented by the H.C. Huntington Company will be sources of pleasure and benefit during the entire stay in Alaska.

We have been well treated by our friends in Seattle and Tacoma. Mr. Kerr, a lawyer, and Mr. Nettleton, to whom we had letters of introduction from their friends in Sandusky, have been able to give us much information and help. They have introduced us to several miners who have just returned from the Yukon country. Major Nettleton has a son in the Northwest Territory, on Henderson creek, and latest reports from him are very encouraging. All the old timers we have met are preparing to go back again, and most of them report the passage into the interior easier than we expected.

Koegle, Sanderson, Deyo and I made a trip to Tacoma last week, and there we found John Lea, Rollin Collins and Aleck Hosmer, all old Sanduskians. They are very enthusiastic over the business conditions and prospects of the northwest, but all retain warm interest in Sandusky and her people.

The weather has been cold and stormy up to yesterday, when the sun came out and gave us a taste Seattle spring. It is about as warm today as you will have anytime in the latter part of April or first of May. Koegle and Sanderson have just come in with violets, pansies and other flowers gathered nearby. Roses bloom here all the year around.

We have had all kinds of fun in this Seattle camp, and I wish you and others who are interested in us could drop in some day and see how comfortable we are. If you were to come in at mealtime you would see 20 of the finest pieces of masticating apparatus at work that ever got grub---well you wouldn't see it, it disappears, vanishes like a summer fog before the noonday sun, as Steward Widman says.

Major Nettleton thought some of inviting the whole party out to his home for dinner, but he happened in at meal time and changed his mind. It was too much for him and he restricted his hospitality to two of us, while extending his good will to all.

If you were to come in a little after midnight, when the orchestra is in full swing, from Deyo's falsetto down to Miller's bass with minor parts taken by Smith Widman, Gleckner and Ross Livengood, you would be carried away by the harmony and grandeur of it all. "Cap" wakes me up now and then to listen to this music, and I assure you it is fine, exhilarating---even maddening at times.

Last night we held an informal musical. Two blind musicians, John O'Brian, an old Sanduskian, and N.P. Sam, a traveling fiddler and singer, came in and gave us a concert, O'Brian accompanying the fiddler on a guitar, and they are a great couple. Sam makes up his verses as he goes along, and I enclose you a copy of a song he made up for our party (Appendix A). All of us are brought into it in some way.[14] Beside this pair we had a mandolin soloist and a dancer. The dancer was a man and gave us a fast clog.

---

[14] The Klondikers Song, *Sandusky Daily Register,* 25 March 1898

We have had one picture taken by a Seattle photographer. It includes all the party except Gleckner, and also a pair of oxen. The picture is good of all we think especially of Thiem and Shay, who, with their guns, knives and axes make a formidable pair. Copies will be sent to you next week.

The oxen were purchased to help us over the Skaguay trail. This is reported to be the best pass and one upon which horses and oxen can be profitably used. At Lake Labarge we shall kill or sell them, as there we are to build boats and start down the river.

Our barque Theobold is guaranteed to leave here not later than March 2, and we shall move aboard her on Tuesday. She is a 1500-ton ship and carries a cargo of hay and lumber to Skaguay.

Will drop you a line at Juneau and Dyea.

Sincerely Yours,

H.R. Huntigton

February 28, 1898

The members of the Sandusky-Klondike party are now on the Pacific Ocean bound northward on a clipper line steamer, which left Seattle Saturday afternoon A final list of supplies having been purchased at Seattle including a yoke of oxen were taken aboard. These will be used to haul the company's supplies over the highest passes on the way to the Klondike.[15]

---

[15] Off For Klondike, *Sandusky Daily Register,* 28 February 1898

Howard Huntington, private secretary to Manager Snevely of the Sandusky-Klondike party, writes the following series of interesting letters to his mother, Mrs. H. C. Huntington. They cover the period from March 8th to 15th and were mailed at Fort Wrangle. Alaska, on the latter date. The Register publishes them through the courtesy of Mrs. Huntington:

Port Alexander,   Tuesday, March 8, 1898

My Dear Mother:

I mailed the first chapter of this letter last night at Alert Bay, where we stopped for water and coal. If we had come up here on a pleasure trip and bent on seeing all there is in it, we couldn't have chosen a better way to come than this old barque.

We never make more than five or six miles an hour and stop whenever the condition of weather or need of water demands it. The town is nothing but a row of Indian huts and a row of Canadian houses skirting the bay, and the only industry of any consequence is the fish canning.

All but a few of the population are Indians, belonging to three tribes. This is their festival season and last night they were holding a "Pot-latch" of blankets. "Pot-latch" means a giving ceremony and is an important custom. In the center of a large hut was blazing a big fire, and the light flickering over the faces of about 100 Indians reclining against the walls and sitting on the ground made a weird picture---and to most of us a strange one.

Near the entrance, in a prominent position, sat the chief, wrapped in a red blanket and watching his children with as calm and indifferent an attitude as any United States court judge ever assumed. On a box near the chief sat the host of the occasion the giver of the blankets, and as his assistant unrolled the cloth and threw it on a mat, the host called the name of him who was to receive it. There was now and then a little grumbling among them, but most of them received the gift without a word. We couldn't understand a word they said, but managed, with gifts of tobacco, to find out the main points of it. Some of them were decked out in war paint and feathers, over the conventional shirt and pants, but they were decidedly peaceable. They had nothing to drink, were very sober and earnest in all their talk and gestures and treated us very civilly. Later in the evening Cap and I went up and called on A. J. Hall, the head of the Indian mission, sent out by the English church. He was very cordial, told us all about his work and showed us his church. I told him I was a press correspondent, on my way to Alaska.

I am glad to say that my impression of a missionary at home and at work is more favorable to the class than those formed by hearing them in our home pulpits.

He says this "Pot-latch" is a system that runs all through the Indian life and assumes very much to our elections and electioneering.

It is giving, always giving, but always with the hope of return. The man who gives away blankets this year expects a gain of 100 per cent on his investment for next year. Each one who received a blanket now gives him back two. Of course, they can't always pay and the blankets and other wealth is apt to accumulate in the hands of a few.

This is the case with every people—the formation of classes—and here they are named and numbered after the feathers of a bird.

Tail feathers are last, and they are constantly striving to rise. Hall says they are well off, have all they want to eat and are perfectly happy. Men have been in there from Alaska offering them big money to go in for packing, but they invariably refuse. What little money they have is made by selling fish to passing boats and by cutting cordwood. We stayed ashore till about 10 o'clock, but the ship remained in the bay till morning. It was my turn on watch last night, and I enjoyed it immensely.

I spent the first three hours of it writing up the journal and the rest on deck getting better acquainted with a young Swede in the crew. The night was fine and clear and as we were lying quietly at anchor the watch was an easy one. This morning we started before I woke up. The tug had been coaled, the anchor raised, and we were well under way when I came on deck.

About 11 o'clock a southeast wind sprang up and we hoisted two topsails. This is the first time we have spread any canvas, as the wind has always been ahead. A southeast wind is nearly a fair wind for us, as we are running about northwest. It soon shifted, however, and by the time we reached the islands at the mouth of Queen Charlotte sound we were running into the teeth of a young gale. Our tug pilot thought best to run into a little bay in one of these islands and anchor, rather than to try to cross the sound in so much wind. He couldn't have found anywhere on the coast as beautiful and snug a little harbor as that in which we are now lying, Alexander Bay. It is about a mile from mouth to head and half that wide, with an average depth of about 15 fathoms. About five miles from the bay, we picked up two Indian canoes. They were trying to row against the wind and having a hard time when we gave them a line. In one were two men and a very plump and jolly looking young squaw, with a pair of snappy black eyes. She was kind enough to smile when I took her picture. They had several halibut in the boats and each fish would weigh about 150 pounds. Later we picked up another canoe and when we reached harbor there were fully one-half dozen with us. We bought some of the fish at one cent a pound and shall have it for breakfast.

Some of the party went ashore to prospect a little for gold or game but found little of either. Wind is blowing hard outside the harbor, and I am glad we did not hit the sound tonight.

So far, we have had a fine trip and beautiful weather all the way. The second mate is sitting across the table reading Monte Cristo. We two and the watch are the only ones awake now, and I think I will turn in and add my little to all this roar and wheeze of snoring around me.

Our bunks are the most comfortable on board and the grub is beyond compare, with which interesting observation I will leave you. Six bells---"11 o'clock—and all's well" has just sounded. Good night.

HOWARD[16]

---

[16] FROM FAR ALASKA, *The Sandusky Daily Register,* 25 March 1898

We are just approaching Fort Wrangle, Alaska, about 250 miles yet from Skagway, and the word has passed around that we would stop, so I shall take the opportunity to drop these lines so that you may know for sure that we are not keeping McGinty company. We expect to reach the destination of this water trip, Skaguay, about next Sunday or Monday. This is a slow old craft, but we think we have not lost anything and we will probably be in much better shape for work when we do get through, by reason of our slowness. The hills show plenty of snow and the air feels bracing. Every member of our party is in perfect health and shows no evidence of homesickness. We all send our best regards to inquiring friends.

J. E. SNEVELY.

Skaguay

From the *Sandusky Register*:

The following letter was received here Wednesday by Mrs. Miller, wife of George J. Miller, who at the time was on his way up to the Klondike gold fields:[17]

On Board Barque Theobald   March 20, 1898

My Dear Wife:

I received your two letters today and I was glad to hear from you again. We arrived at Skaguay all right. Captain Snevely, Sanderson and myself took a walk of ten miles up the trail and back again. We saw about 500 men on the trail and some woman. Tomorrow we unload our cargo and move up the trail. Don't believe everything you see in the papers. The papers at Seattle seem to hatch up all kinds of stories

Today we saw one woman driving some goats; another had oxen, and another had saddle mules, while others had horses. Dogs were worth $30 at Seattle and here you can get them for 25 cents and even less. You can see what a difference it would make if you were to buy six or eight. We went up the river trail this morning and saw some large mountains. We are going over the trail all right. We are not going over the dangerous passes and we thought we would never get here. The boat was slow. The population of this town is about 5000. Some of the houses are very small and are made of logs.

---

[17] On Alaska's Frozen Soil, *Norwalk Daily Reflector,* 7 April 1898

Carpenters here get $5 a day. We saw the happiest lot of fellows on the trail, and they were making good time. There is a theatre here and also a church.

Sandwiches are worth 15 cents or two for 25 cents. Mr. Sanderson was our cook, and we are going to have Judge Shay and Dell Deyo, so Captain Snevely says. Tell Albert that we have three instruments- -a guitar, violin and mandolin. We have but two players one for the guitar and one for the mandolin. Howard Huntington and Andy Meinzer are the musicians, but there are several in the party on board the ship who play the violin.

We lay at anchor at Bernier Bay Saturday and Sunday and that delayed us over four days. One or two of the boys have gone to Dyea for our mail. It is stated in the newspapers that there is a disease common here from the effects of which many people are dying all of which is untrue. Gold has been discovered at Fort Wrangle and at Bernier Bay where they have a mine and a stamp mill and employ about 60 men. I heard that a big strike has been made about 40 miles from here on the way to the Klondike, but I cannot tell if there is any truth in the statement. They are paying $2.50 a day here to men building a corduroy road on the side of the mountain.

I don't know when I will write again, as I cannot tell where we are going as yet. Last Sunday we shot a hair seal, but he sank out of sight. We have not seen a bear or a deer to shoot at since we have been up here. Tell Cowan that if he had a team here, he could make about $15 per day hauling stuff over the trail. You may send your next letter to Skaguay. Give all my best regards.

From your loving husband,

George J. Miller

The following letter was received by the *Sandusky Daily Register* from Howard Huntington, secretary to Captain Snevely of the Sandusky-Klondike.[18]

Mouth Skaguay Canyon,   March 27, 1898

J.C. Schuefler, Sandusky, Ohio

Dear Sir,

This is Sunday, so the calendar says but you would never guess it from a look at this canyon. Every man on the street has been working just as hard today as he did yesterday, and so it goes here seven days a week.

The Theobald landed us in Skaguay harbor last Monday morning after a voyage of nineteen days---too long by at least a week, but there was no help for it, and no one to blame but a slow tug and a slower pilot. But here we are at last all in good health and all bucking the canyon trail to the best of our strength. We were delayed in getting landed by heavy winds and it was Wednesday night before we had the satisfaction of seeing all the outfit up to camp No. 1, a couple of miles from high water mark.

We had fine weather all the way from Seattle, Queen Charlotte Sound giving us the only touch of a rough sea on the trip. Four stops were made and at three of them we were able to post letters, so that our friends at home have been pretty fully informed before this letter reaches you. The crew on the Theobold was small and our party turned in and helped at every possible chance. We had a hand

---

[18] In Skaguay Pass, *Sandusky Daily Register,* 12 April 1898

in the sailing of the vessel, while moving and when anchored it was our men that turned in and got fresh water and moved the cargo. Between the 60 passengers and the cattle aboard we ran short of water rather often. The only way to get more was to fill the ship's longboat from some stream near our anchorage, row it out to the ship and then pump it into the tanks by hand. Dell, our bear killer had a chance to distinguish himself in this work. He had the care of the nozzle end of the hose one night and instead of directing it into the tank he ran it into a hole that led down to our bunks. A few wet blankets was the result and if the captain hadn't come along he would have sunk the ship, or at least drowned this party.

Among the passengers we found several musicians and with our instruments we were able to get up a very fair trio, a mandolin, guitar and violin. We serenaded every quarter of the ship till they must have grown tired of the old pieces we played, but it served to kill many of the hours that our pilot lost.

At Skaguay we found the wharves all crowded and the cargo had to be put on lighters and towed ashore and when the tide went out it left them high and dry on the beach. The four or five hours between high and low tide were used to haul the goods in wagons from the lighter up above the highest tide mark. Our 25 tons of stuff came off on the first lighter. It was all in good shape except a few bags of flower and feed that had been laid on coal in the vessel and been dampened. We had hard work getting it all off the lighter before high tide time but worked hard and managed to get away in time. At our first camp we had but two tents pitched and worked out of doors. Speaking of working reminds me that we made an addition to our party before leaving the boat. A Mr. Graham and wife and horse were traveling our way with the usual amount of baggage and an agreement was made by which they go with us as far as they like

Mr. Grahm and his horse doing their share of the pulling and Mrs. G. spending her time cooking for us. It is a fine thing for us and also for them and let me tell you we are faring out of sight. We need to, for a man can't do this sort of work and live on faith.

On Thursday we moved most of our stuff about one mile over a very fair road-the lower part of the river. The next camp was set five miles further on, near the mouth of the canyon, where we are now. Tents are thick all around us and for a half mile up and down the road. The population of this canvas town is constantly changing, each habitant moving up the trail as fast as possible. And that possible isn't very fast, let me tell you. The terrors of these few miles have not been swelled in the telling. It is just what we looked for--- a hard proposition, and the only way of doing it is to keep bucking, and buck till it is done. All day yesterday the whole party has been busy, most of them toiling up and down a mile stretch with a pack of fifty pounds on their backs, while the oxen and Graham's horse worked with sleds. We are making fine progress with that 25 tons of grub and hands are doing well. There are many faint hearts on the trail but none in this party. Many sell out and go home, but I believe every man in this crowd will stay by the outfit till it grows cold in Hades and we can skate home on the ice.

The weather is queer. At night it freezes hard and continues cold till the sun gets high enough to shine down into the canyon and then it melts fast, so that by four in the afternoon the trail is very wet.

I have taken several pictures today which will give you some idea of this canyon town and our own camp. It is a wonderful sight, and no one can picture it till he sees it. The road all day long is crowded to its utmost with all sorts of people and all kinds of beasts of burden. It is like some of the pictures of the Exodus, and a thousand times more interesting because we are in it. In the canon proper the trail is very narrow and rocky and often gets blocked with horses and men. The ice on the river is broken in many places and the least misstep on the part of an animal; either man or beast will land him in a cold stream. Many horses or dogs die from the work or are killed by a fall into the stream. One surprising thing is the good nature evident among these prospectors. You hear very little cursing or grumbling; all are happy as clams in high water, but all working hard. It is great and I wish you could see it.

It is very hard to get mail at Skaguay and I wish you would impress it on our friends that they must address all letters to J. E. Snevely. Agt. A.C.M. Co. and the individuals name in the lower left-hand corner of the envelope. We shall be within reach of Skaguay for six weeks more and mail is precious here.

All the boys send regards.

Sincerely yours,

H.R. HUNTINGTON

The following letter was received by the *Sandusky Daily Register* from Howard Huntington, secretary to Captain Snevely of the Sandusky-Klondike party.[19]

Camp number II   Saturday, April 2, 1898.

This is camp life with a vengeance. Ten of us are crowded around a Yukon stove, reclining on clothing, bags, sleds, anything that can furnish a seat the size of a three-cent piece, all talking at once and Miller banging a Chinese dance on the stove. We have all been working hard, early and late, and seven days in the week, since we came ashore a week ago Thursday. For all except the cook's assistant and the bull punchers, the work has been packing, toiling up and down Porcupine hill, over the rocks and through rivers of water and mud, and always with a burden of from 50 to 100 pounds strapped to the shoulders. Not a foot in the crowd that hasn't been blistered and not a temper that hasn't been tried, till it either bent or broke, and still, we are 20 men and all on good terms. We have seen many a party break up, each member taking his share of the outfit and going his way alone, but in spite of many premature prophesies to the contrary, we, the A.C.M. Co., are 20 and eat and sleep under the same canvas. The work is hard---harder even than we looked for---but the life is glorious, free and wonderful to men who have been tied down to shops and desks as most of these have been.

In my last letter I gave you some account of our progress up to last Monday. We were then camped in the lower canyon and packing

---

[19] Up and Over Skaguay Pass, *Sandusky Daily Register,* 16 April 1898

our goods from camp to the foot of Porcupine hill. We thought that was a pretty stiff piece of work and a climb over a mile of boulders and across ice bridges, where a slip meant a cold bath or perhaps worse, made every man of us ready and glad to crawl into his sleeping bag as soon as supper was over. We have struck this trail about ten days late, for it is wearing out and breaking up very fast. Every day it gets worse, and we have more need to hurry. The fact is we have to catch up with the weather. The higher we go the colder it will get, and when once we are up beyond this thaw we can begin to sled instead of packing. For a few days at the beginning of this warm spell it froze enough at night to repair the days thaw, but now things have changed. It doesn't freeze at night and each morning the road is softer and the ice is thinner than the day before. Our second pack was from the foot of Porcupine hill to a cache about a half mile over the hill. This was tougher than the first. The path winds around the hill and is very steep. Here the footing was very insecure and not one of us got through a day without several downs, and a down in that mud--mud that runs in rivers-- mud that forms puddles of a foot in depth---mud that stuck where it struck and left a taste for a week afterward---was something to make a week man quail. At the top of that hill was a breathing spot where every packer rested his load against a log or a rock and watched the rest toiling up toward him. From this point one could get a view that almost repaid him for his work the first time he saw it. There below him several hundred feet, he could see at crowded times a busier scene than any other thorofare in the United States could present. Imagine Columbus avenue changed into a river and ice coated, dotted with rocks that stand out sometimes 30 feet; the brick stores replaced by walls of granite 200 feet in height; a path rounding in and out among the boulders and on that path a half thousand mules horses and oxen, several hundred dogs hitched to sleds, and a thousand men, some with packs on their backs and others driving and yelling at horses and dogs and you will have some idea of what that canyon looks like. Sometimes there will be a dozen horses in the river at once, all surrounded by men trying to pull them out, and if this happens where the trail is narrow there is a blockade and a line several hundred yards in length will form in a very few moments. The best way to take an outfit over this trail is to have it packed by professional packers. These men own trains of horses or mules all the way from 2 to 50 in number, and they make the trip from Skaguay to the summit and back in a day. If the goods are well covered, they go through in fine condition, providing none of the brutes fall or get into the river. The rate of freight from Skaguay is 5 or 6 cents per pound with these people and they do plenty of business. They might be said to own the trail for when they come along, they can be heard for a long distance, the driver--generally a man to five horses-- yelling and swearing at such a rate and in such a tongue as no man ever heard outside this canyon. But of course, only a few of these prospective millionaires can afford to pay the price of having their goods packed over. Hand packing is easy on the goods but hard on the men. Sledding is terrible on both. The sleds are dragged through mud and water till the load is soaked through and ruined. Much of the food that goes through this slough on sleds can never be of any use to its owner, but still, it goes through. Our outfit is in fine condition at this writing, and Captain Snevely is devoting himself to keeping it so.

A burro is considered the best animal for packing here. They carry as much as the largest horse or mule and live on faith and works. If they fall into a hole they can be pulled out by the ears about as easy as a jack rabbit. The funniest and slowest pair is one of those little burros driven by a Dutchman from Frisco. He is 40 years old and the ass a little older. He goes jogging along at a snail's pace poking the ass with a little stick. No matter how slow the beast the master never gets hot---he is as slow as the ass. If Mr. Burro wants a meal he stops at some miner's outfit and eats hay out of a bale or bites a hole in a sack of oats. Dutchy never interferes till the owner of the hay throws a club or stone at the beast, when Dutchy makes a great show of trying to urge on his ass. I shall get a picture of him before I reach the summit.

This camp No. 2 of ours is about halfway between Skaguay and the summit, and we are doing our best to get up on the solid snow. It is pitched on the ice and now and then we can hear the ice crack beneath us. It is six feet thick, however, and there is little danger of its breaking through. We have all four tents up and Graham is camped just south of us. Mr. and Mrs. Graham are a great help. He works his nag and himself from morning till night, and she runs the kitchen in such a way that not a man has complained of the food up to this time.

Sunday,   April 3, 1898

Today we are taking a rest. We got eight inches of very wet snow last night, and some of the dangerous spots in the river above us have broken through. They will have to be bridged before they can be used for horses or oxen and there are men at work at it now. We are in such a place that we can get onto Brackett's road at any time and be sure of getting across. This Brackett's Road is a private enterprise, and a toll of two cents a pound is charged on all goods taken through the gate. There has been much discussion and a little violent trouble over that road, as it was doubted the owner had a charter, but he has the United States marshal back of him now and is receiving toll from all hands. We may escape all or part of it by hand packing our goods through but shall have to pay at least once for taking the oxen through. Everybody is glad of this days' rest. It gives a chance to dry clothes and talk over our chances and troubles. It is the general opinion that we are doing well---making fine progress--and Captain Snevely assures us that we shall be over the summit in ten days. The lower trail---the one we are on now--- will be worse tomorrow than ever before, unless it freezes tonight. Most of the boys are writing letters but a few are gathered about the parlor stove and just at present Deacon Widman is telling us what he can remember now of the war. A discussion has arisen over the Deacons ability to remember anything he did at the close of the war---he was five years old at the time--- Pat McCrystal, our politician , takes a leading part in the argument.

Barring one case of neuralgia and a few sore hands and feet, the crowd are perfectly well and will go to work in the morning. The day's task is always apportioned to the strength of the weakest member, so that no man does more than he ought. Some are able to finish their part before the rest and Pat and Miller are big hearted enough to help others when their task is done. That is the sort of spirit that holds this party together, while others break up. I send you a quill from a porcupine killed on Porcupine hill.

I have received letters from home twice this week---two last Wednesday and two yesterday. A letter here is worth a thousand at Harvard, for when a man does a day's work here he feels as though he had earned some such pleasure. Continue to address your letters to Skaguay. We shall be within reach of that post office until May 1.

With love to all,

HOWARD

The first gold nugget was received yesterday from the Sandusky-Klondike party by the local company which sent the hardy men to the far north in quest of fortune. It is a pretty little chunk of rich yellow metal as pure as the snowflakes in Alaska's clear air, and worth several dollars. The first nugget means something, and of course, every friend of every member in the party will want to see it. To give all this opportunity it will be placed in the display window of Parsons & Irvine's shoe store on Columbus Avenue today and kept on exhibition for a week.[20]

The following bright and newsy letter was received last night by J.C. Scheufler, secretary of the Alaska Co-operative Mining Co. from H.R. Huntington, secretary to Captain Snevely.[21]

Camp No. 4. White Pass,   April 11

Mr. J. C. Scheufler, Sandusky, Ohio

Dear Sir:

During the two weeks that have passed since I wrote you, we have advanced just six miles on our way to the summit. This distance was made in two moves each of about three miles. We are

---

[20] First Gold Nugget, *Sandusky Daily Register,* 16 April 1898
[21] Slippery Mountains of The White Pass, *Sandusky Daily Register,* 29 April 1898

camped now a quarter mile south of White Pass where the toll gate is situated. There the toll road joins the old trail and all passing through with pulling or packing animals of any kind have to pay tribute to Brackett[22] and his United States marshals. The only way to get by without paying is to pull or pack our goods through by hand and this is done by a large majority of prospectors. The outfits are hauled up by horses and oxen, just as ours has been, to within a quarter mile of the gate, and there they are cached to be packed over beyond the gate a half-mile. There the oxen take them again and haul them to the summit, where they are sorted and stacked up for the inspection of the Canadian customs officials

There is some justice in the demands of this road builder. He has been enterprising and persevering enough to construct a highway from Skaguay to the summit---or rather to within three miles of the summit---and most of the road has been cut out of solid rock or made of logs. It should make White Pass the popular summer trail if the toll charge is not put too high. At present it is two cents per pound if the road is used all the way from town or half a cent if only used from White Pass to the summit. The chief objection raised is to the fact that he has put the gate at the junction of the old trail and his road, and tried at first to collect the two cent rate whether a man came all the way from Skaguay on his road or used the river trail. For a while the travelers defied his men and refused to pay anything, but he got a few United States marshals out here and now collects from all but hand packers. We shall pay toll on only a few tons of our goods---mostly on the camp outfit.

---

[22] George Brackett began building a toll road from Skaguay to the summit in 1897, charging $10 per wagon to use it. When the stampeders objected to the fees, he called in the U.S. Army to enforce them.

We thought, when we had passed Porcupine Hill and the lower canyon that the worst of our trials were over, but it seems that was only a beginning. Every hill we come to---and there are many of them--- is worse than the one before it, and the road from the toll gate to the summit is about as steep as climbing a tree. The hill just behind us over which the oxen dragged our freight was perhaps the hardest of all on the teams. A freeze at night made it very slippery in the morning and no horse or ox could go up it with over 600 pounds behind him. Our boys went over it without any serious mishap, but they did have one fall. They were pulling up the hill, each with a loaded sled behind him, when a horse ahead of them slipped and fell. The weight of his load dragged him back down the steep decline at such a rate that before our boys could clear the road, the horse and load were upon them and all three sled-loads with the two oxen and horse went sliding and rolling down that hill and piled into a good-sized wreck at the foot of it. I didn't see the mix-up, but they tell me it was highly exciting.

So far, we have kept our outfit in very good condition. It is hard to do this for the sacks will get wet in spite of every precaution. Much of the grub that goes through will never be fit for anything, so mud and water-soaked is it. The mud is gathered in the canyons where the sleds tip over on the rocks and are often dragged some yards before the horse can be stopped and the sled righted.

I have taken a number of pictures lately which will give you some idea of the canyons and what our camps look like. I shall send the pictures to Mr. Carl Osburg who will develop them, and no doubt have the work on exhibition. One of them --I hope it is clear--- shows us all seated about the kitchen tent eating dinner. The weather is warm enough for eating out of doors, strange as it may seem to you, and there have been very few days so far that this could not be done. At mealtime every man forgets his troubles, regains his temper---too easily lost at this kind of work--- and gives himself up to the full enjoyment of his bacon and biscuit, the two staple articles of food. After dinner there is always time for a pipe and a talk. This talk is a terror for some, a pleasure for most of us. No one escapes and many a roar of laughter rings through these canons at the expense of some member who has provoked ridicule. After supper most of us are too tired to care for this kind of amusement and we either go to bed or retire to the "saloon tent" or drying room, where a pipe can be enjoyed in silence, or we can have music. The saloon tent is a great institution. It gives us a place to loaf in bad weather as well as furnishing a room for drying clothes. It is well heated by a Yukon stove and large enough to hold a gathering of the entire party in times of council.

We have three sleeping tents since the last purchase. Eight in the large one and six in each of the other two. Here the sleeping bags are spread on spruce boughs and boards and with four pair of blankets and a hair mattress to each pair of men we manage to rest very comfortably. It is a great life we lead, free and easy, perhaps a little rough; it would seem to some of you, but one that can't help but do us all good. Most of us are gaining in weight on this work and fare, particularly Dell and Shay.

Koegle has just come in with the news that all our goods are past the toll gate and we have saved at least $200 by packing through. We shall move tomorrow over to Log Cabin, 12 miles from here. Will write you again from that point.

Respectfully yours,

    H R HUNTINGTON

Jay Livengood, a member of the Sandusky-Klondike party and well known in this city and community, writes the following letter to his mother, Mrs. Livengood, Sand Hill.[23]

White Pass,   April 12

   Dear Mother

   I thought I would write a few lines to you to let you know what we are doing, and what shape we are in. All are feeling good but a little tired. Tomorrow we will get all our goods to the summit, and then we will move to Log Cabin. That is 16 miles. The captain has his papers, and we will go right through without any trouble. We are getting along nicely, and everything is running smooth. We have been hauling to the summit. In four miles the rise is 2,000 feet. I tell you she is a peach. We have been hauling on the snow and it is from six to ten feet deep and on the trail the snow drifted as high as 250 feet, and we have been hauling all of our goods over it, and from the summit north the ground slopes 1,000 miles in. We are all well and the boys are making so much noise that I can't write nor think of anything to write about. I got your letter April 4 and one from Carrie and one from Bertha, all at the same time, and was glad to hear from you all and want all to keep writing.

   Tell Carrie to write again and when I get to Dawson, I will have time to write to you all and I can tell you more about it. Tell Bertha to write I was glad to hear from her. Write often. When I get a Sunday to myself, I will write you all a long letter and tell you all about Alaska. Tell Charlie if he could only haul hay out here, he could

---

[23] Over White Pass, *Sandusky Daily Register,* 7 May 1898

make all kinds of money. Hay on the summit is worth 20 cents a pound and oats the same, and at Lake Bennett it is as much again.

Well, I will quit for this time, and you address your letter to Skaguay for a while. Tell the boys I send my best.

April 14

We are at Log Cabin, 18 miles from White Pass. We started at 8 am and broke a trail to the summit. During the night the snow fell eight inches and in two places on the trail they had snow slides. One struck the Ford Hotel and smashed it to slivers, but no one was hurt, but three mules and eight goats were lost. Snow was piled up 40 feet high on the trail. We are getting along nicely, and the next move will be to Lake Bennett and there is where we will build our boats. It will take some time.

Sunday April, 17

At Log Cabin today has been a day of rest for me. Yesterday I put in 20 hours and today I have been taking a bath and mending my clothes and sewing on buttons. Will start for the summit at 6 tonight. That is 16 miles. Will get back with my load tomorrow about noon. I have five more trips to make and then I will be through with the oxen for a while. We will get all our goods over to Lake Lindeman and there we will commence to build our boats and as soon as the ice is gone, we will go too. There is lots of snow here yet. We are camped out on six feet of the white down, and we lay our beds on the Alaska feathers--- that is the small branches of the fir trees. I want to say to you they are not so bad as one might think, but of course they are not as soft as one of your feather beds, but with six feet of snow and eight inches of boughs under you and four good blankets for two men you can sleep good after working from

15 to 20 hours, and you would not know you was in the land or on the ground. I have just built a little box for my paper and books and my little Bible, which I think more of than anything I have got and when I cannot think of anything to do then I get the little book out and read for a while, and I want to say to you it is lots of comfort to me. Today I have looked through it.

Perry has called for dinner, and I must go and eat and go to bed, for at 6 I leave for the summit, and I ought to have been in bed all day. So goodbye. Now for my dinner.

April 18

Almost too tired to write but will try to say something. We left camp last night at 7:30 and got there at 2 and at 2:30 we were on our road back with a ton each. Got back in time for dinner making the round trip of 32 miles at one stretch, and it was a tiresome job all night in a blinding snowstorm. Some of the time we could hardly find the trail but made the trip all right. Tell Joe that he ought to be here to skin dead horses and mules, for on the White and Chilkoot the horses lay dead by the hundreds. Each day from two to ten are killed. I saw one shot this morning because it was so tired it could scarcely move. The man unhooked the horse from the sleigh and tried to lead it and it did not step up to suit him and out came his pistol and down went the horse on the trail.

There are thousands going down the lakes and one in five is a woman dressed in men's clothes, with their husbands, pulling a sleigh like a man. The other day I saw a woman drawing 700 pounds on a hand sleigh. She was dressed in trousers of fur, a black cap and a red sweater. She was a sight for her trousers were about four feet wide. Today I saw one that was dressed right in line. She had on knee breeches made of corduroy with buttons on the legs, and coat and vest to match, and a nice ribbon tied in her hair. A big belt with a lot of cartridges in it and a gun was about her waist. She wore a big white hat. She did not look as warm as the one with fur trousers. Well I am so sleepy I can hardly write, so I will quit for this time and next week will be at the lake and then will write you again. Tell all of my friends that I am on top yet---that is on top of the snow and will try to keep on top. Goodbye with love to all.

PS --- You can mail your letters to Skaguay for eight weeks or so. Maybe we will not get our boats done before that time and if we should we will have them forwarded to Dawson. I now get all the letters that are written to me. Last week I got five in a bunch, so I know that all my friends have not forgotten me.

JAY

Letter from George J. Miller[24]

Albert Bergmoser has received a letter from Geo. Miller, of the Sandusky-Klondike party, of which the following is part:

Well, we are living good. For breakfast we have bacon, bread and coffee: for dinner we have coffee, bread and bacon: for supper bread, bacon and coffee. So you see we have changes. But if we don't have a wash day pretty soon, we won't have a change of shirts or underwear.

---

[24] Hard Work on the Trail, *The Sandusky Star,* 15 May 1898

The boys in camp worked hard the last month packing goods on their backs and hauling sleighs. Up to last Friday Charles Smith and I went with our oxen to the summit to haul our goods to Log Cabin, a distance of 32 miles for the round trip. We would start from here in the evening and get back the next forenoon, if we had good luck. We have been on the road as high as 20 hours on a trip, and it isn't very warm on these night trips either.

We had to walk all the way and we took all types of tumbles in the canyons. You never saw such roads as there are here---around rocks, over rocks, and a shoot ten feet down with a thump. I don't care how well you tie the loads on the head sleigh and trailers they will fall off or capsize in spite of all you can do. We were about tuckered out when we got home and could hardly climb the hill that leads to the log cabin. You can see dead dogs and horses all along the trail.

Say, is Co. B called out? How about the war, is there any truth in the report? If you can't read this letter lay it onto cold fingers in a cold tent, because the air is pretty cold today. You might address my letter thus:

Capt. J.E. Snevely,

Care A.C.M. Co.,

Skaguay, Alaska.

Bennett City

Below is Howard Huntington's letter for the New York Post:[25]

I am in a sort of advance camp here on the lake, and it gives me a chance to try my hand at nearly everything pertaining to camp life. I have to cook for four Alaskan appetites three times a day and make coffee for fifteen more at noon. I am in charge of the last cache we shall make before starting down the Yukon. My tent is pitched on rock bottom and surrounded by walls of snow from 12 to 15 feet in height, so I am well sheltered from the cold south winds that blow almost constantly across the lake at this season.

I moved over here from Log Cabin a distance of nine miles on Sunday, and that night camped here with one other member of our company. We had a half day of snow shoveling and wood cutting before we could put up a tent and stove, but when at last we did get the tent pitched we were as comfortable as I ever was in Perkins Hall, Cambridge.

We are as comfortable now and are probably the worst of this trip. Cowan is snow-blind today. He is the first victim, and I hope, the last. The attack is very painful, and one who has it can do nothing but sit in a tent with face covered and cuss his luck.

We shall be in camp here till the ice goes out, and old inhabitants say that will not be for a month. It is a beautiful spot---a lake surrounded by the snow-covered mountains and dotted all along by

---

[25] Klondikers at Lake Lindeman, *Norwalk Daily Reflector,* 17 May 1898

moving trains of Klondikers. The trails from Dyea and Skaguay meet at this point, and it is a busy place. Sails are used on sleds, and we often see one man and a sail pulling a ton of goods over the lake. A canyon joins Lindeman and Bennett lakes and at the latter quite a city has been started---all canvas of course, and all to come down at the breaking of the ice.

H.R. Huntington

HOW SANDUSKY PARTY'S BIG SCOW WAS BUILT

From the *Sandusky Journal.*

The following graphic letter from Howard Huntington to the New York Post, for which he is correspondent, is of date previous to some others which have been published in these columns. It is very entertainingly written however, and so well describes the building of the big scow upon which the party will make the trip down the Yukon, and trials of other subjects that will be of interest to every friend of the party, that is herewith printed in full: [26]

Bennett City   May 25, 1898

Since my last letter conditions in and about this canvas city have changed, affecting in some degree our plans for departure. The river between lakes Lindeman and Bennett has for several days past been

---

[26] The Klondike Trail, *The Norwalk Daily Reflector,* 18 July 1898

carrying down tons and tons of honey-combed ice that tell of the opening of Lindeman, and warn the impatient prospector that he must soon be ready to load his boat and once more take up his journey toward Dawson City and the land of gold. The trails between Bennett City and the coast are now about deserted, and only a hurrying newsboy or mail-carrier can be seen picking his perilous way over rocks, boulders and waterfalls, where a month ago an eager throng of humanity toiled from daylight to dark, all bent on reaching the lakes in time to start with "the rush".

That rush, however, does not start all in one hour nor one day. Parties have been leaving this point every day during the last week, but most of them were stopped by the ice on Lake Bennett, and the few who did manage to find a narrow channel in those dangerous floating fields stand a good chance of having their boats crushed and lives lost further down the lake. Bennett is very much like a river, narrow and abounding in treacherous currents, particularly at Windy Arm and West Arm, where all are likely to meet heavy winds and to need a good stretch of open water in order to keep the boats off the rocks on either shore, and those who try to cross the lake when it is full of drift ice do so at terrible risk to life and outfit. In spite of the danger, they continue to push on, some in boats not fit for any sort of navigation and built on such lines as to be unmanageable in swift water. Many of these men have never handled a boat before and one can't help wondering how they are ever going to make the trip, with their scant experience and in such craft as they build.

The prevailing style of boat for a party of three is the "shary" with caulked seams, about 25 feet long and from three to six feet beam. The bottom is generally very narrow, and when empty they are about as hard to sit in as a birch-bark canoe. For a large party of ten or twenty a scow is best, and they are made large enough to afford living and sleeping room, besides the space required for the outfits. Our boat, a scow with twenty-six feet bottom, thirty-eight feet overall, and about twelve feet beam, was launched last Saturday afternoon. She has been pronounced by many the best boat of her class in Bennett City yards. We were fortunate in getting only the best timber available, and all dry stuff. Many have used green lumber and suffered the discouragement of seeing their boat seams open up as the lumber dried out. The seasoned stuff swells in water and makes a tight boat.

On our scow we have built a galley just forward of the mast, where two stoves will be set up and two cooks do their best to keep the rest of the party in good humor during the trip to Dawson. Just aft of the mast and over the cargo we have laid six double bunks, so that twelve of us can sleep at one time. Then, of course we have our poop-deck, upon which those of us who understand sailing will handle the sweep. We expect a fair wind most of the trip, as the prevailing winds at this season are from the south, and with a 16x18 tent-fly spread for a sail, we should make good time. After Lake Labarge and the rapids are past we shall stop for nothing; we can eat and sleep aboard ship, and all the twenty- four hours will be light enough for sailing

The work of getting out logs and whipsawing was not half so hard as we expected. Reports reached us as far back as White Pass of the scarcity of timber around these lakes, and we had about decided that the Bennett City sawmill would be our only resource. On the west side of Lindeman, where the timber is green, this milling company has obtained a grant of all the timber for miles back from the lake, and they guard it very carefully. On the east side there has been a forest fire within the past four or five years, and any logs that come down from the hills in that section are well seasoned. Back into this burnt-over timber we took our ox and sixteen men, and within a week had logs enough cut and dragged down over the horse- trail to make all the boats we could need. The party was then divided into river-men and whip-sawyers, and with both gangs working steadily we soon had enough lumber to start our carpenter work on the scow. It was all managed so easily and the sawing so quickly finished that we were surprised at ourselves and inclined to laugh at the fears we had before starting the work.

So,it has been during the entire journey from Skaguay. We were told in Seattle that this party would never stick together, and as for the trail, the stories we heard of it in the states were far more horrible than the reality. I do not say that it is an easy trip; but I do say that any healthy man or woman can make it who will just "push on" and remember only that the lakes must be reached.

After the boats are built there comes a rest of a couple of weeks for those who crossed the mountains with us, a longer time for those ahead of us, and plenty of amusement can be found in Bennett City. Of course, it is a wide-open town in some ways but not in the sense of our western boom towns. There are saloons and gambling dens, but they are well controlled, and a street brawl or open disturbance is a rare occurrence, so vigilant are the Canadian mounted police. Stationed at this point there have been at times as many as 15,000 people camped on less than a square mile of ground about the head of Bennett, and today there is scarcely a spot on either side of the main street where one could find room to pitch a tent, and yet a dog fight is the nearest approach to trouble we ever see.

Nearly all have the same goal in view, and each one is more than willing to help his neighbor attain it. A man in trouble here is sure of aid; if he wishes to launch his boat he has only to say when, and he will have more assistance than he can use. If he strikes a rock coming down from Lindeman to Bennett, there will be no lack of men to wade into the river to work him off. Last night a small boat capsized just above our camp, and an outfit came floating downstream. We rescued part of it and the rest was picked up by a boatman farther down the river, who demanded $1.50 for his services. The money was paid, but within a half hour a large crowd had gathered and elected a committee to call upon the boatman for the return of the money. In case he refused, the committee informed him that the crowd would come over and wait upon him. He returned the money and the crowd dispersed. So it goes--- they will not allow an unfortunate man to be swindled.

The temperature has a wide range here. Yesterday it registered 102 degrees out of doors and 120 in the kitchen. It was too warm to work with comfort. Today, however, it is cold and raw; thermometer down to 40, and a stiff wind blowing from the south, which makes a warm coat welcome.

H.R.Huntington

From the *Sandusky Journal*

Several letters have been received in the city by relatives and friends of the Sandusky Klondike party. According to latest advices they left the camp at Lake Bennett May 30 on the voyage down the Yukon to Dawson City, which, under favorable circumstances would require about fifteen days, it is estimated.

No more letters could be mailed by the party until they reached Dawson City, and none are now expected here before August 1.

The following extracts were taken by permission from a private letter from Howard Huntington:[27]

Bennett City   May 25, 1898

At about 3 o'clock this afternoon we were hailed from across the river by an old man with long flowing hair, a wide sombrero, and trapper's jacket, who had just come out from Skaguay and brought 39 letters for our party. He had brought them from the postmaster at Skaguay and paid five cents each for each, and now demanded a profit of twenty cents each for his trouble. We paid his price after a slight remonstrance. Three of them were mine and it required all the rest of the afternoon to digest them.

It is now half-past twelve--midnight--- and I can just see to read this letter outdoors. It is warm and I went out to make the experiment.

(Unnamed person) is on watch tonight, but he lies snoring lustily on a pile of rocks back of the stove. I shall have to wake him for I need rest in order to be up and at work by seven. Work is light now. Our scow, the finest in Bennett yards, is complete and lies at anchor in the river near us. Sanderson and his boat building gang are at work on several small prospecting boats, and when they are finished---probably by Sunday--- we shall load up and start downstream. We can't go fast as the ice will block us, but we hope

---

[27] Now at Dawson City, *The Norwalk Daily Reflector,* 27 June 1889

to make Windy Arm, where we can find better timber and perhaps fish and game. Lindeman is breaking up fast and the ice is unsafe on Bennett.

Bennett City,   May 30.1898

It is a cold raw day, and the thermometer is down to 40 degrees, and a stiff wind is blowing from the south. The temperature has a wide range here. Yesterday it registered 102 degrees outdoors and 120 degrees in the kitchen. It was too warm to work comfortably and today it is too cold to be without a warm coat. We leave here right after dinner and in a few days shall be at the rapids. Our scow is tight and staunch as a drum, and we shall make the run in safety. From Dawson I shall mail you a long letter, explaining our summer plans and telling all about the rapids.

Love to all, once more and the last time till we are beyond the rapids and then my mail will travel 7,000 miles to reach you. Do not worry; we shall sit around the same old fire once more, I am sure, and when we do what stories we will tell.

   Howard

Sylvester Widman, Of Fremont, who is with the Sandusky Klondike party, has written an interesting letter to his wife, which was published in the Fremont-Messenger Thursday. It is as follows:[28]

---

[28] Klondike Letter, *The Freemont Messenger,* 5 July 1898

Bennett City B.C.,   May 29, 1898

My Dear Wife:

--I will again take the opportunity to write you a few lines and let you know that I am well and in good spirits.

We are now ready to sail for Dawson City. We have our boats all completed. We will kill our last ox in the morning and start on Tuesday.

There are thousands of boats being built here, of all sizes and forms. Some put me in mind of a store box, and some are very fine. There are some fine steamboats being built here that will run from here to Dawson City. If a man doesn't want to build a boat, he can get passage from here to Dawson City for $35. There are about 35,000 people going to the gold fields this way, and I don't think there will be over 30,000 in all coming to this country.

I never told you how the horses are used in this country when the people are through with them, they sell them, or if they cannot sell them, they take a gun and shoot them in the head. There are about 2500 dead horses on this trail. I tell you; they will make a fine odor when it gets warm.

Our Captain was appointed as United States surveyor, and our lawyer was appointed notary public by the governor of Alaska, so you see that if we find good claims it will not take us very long to stake out our claims and make out the papers for them.

This will be the last time I will write from here. We expect to be in Dawson City inside of ten days. We expect to stay in Dawson a few days and get our mail and see how they mine gold there, and then go to Circle City, which is 300 miles from Dawson. When you write again address the letter this way:

J.E. Snevely,

Circle City, Alaska

I will close for this time and write more the next time. My best love to you and all yours

Very Truly,

S. Widman.

Mr. Widman sends a pencil sketch of the" Sandusky Boy's" boat. It is 50 feet long and 12 feet beam. The deck is pretty well occupied by tents and the kitchen. From the mast float the stars and stripes and a pennant bearing the inscription, "Sandusky Headquarters".

The Yukon Voyage

The New York Post published the following graphic letter from Howard R. Huntington, one of the Sandusky Klondikers, descriptive of the trip down the Yukon River: [29]

Dawson City N.W.T.   June 13

We arrived here yesterday at noon all in good health and with our outfit in perfect condition. The scow Buckeye has proved worthy of her builders, having come out unscathed after a voyage of 600 miles over lakes and rivers where many boats have been wrecked and many a miner has lost both outfit and life. It has taken us 12 days to make the trip, as we didn't hurry, save where there was danger of drifting ashore or onto a rock, and allowed the current to bring us most of the way.

The run from Bennett to Dawson is well worth the trouble and work of bring an outfit over the pass from Skaguay. We have had fine weather all the way, a fair wind coming over the lakes, and a four to six mile current in the rivers. We left Bennett on the afternoon of May 30, amid the cheers of a thousand miners, who were soon to follow us, and drifted down Bell River and out into Lake Bennett, where a fair wind was soon carrying us along at a

[29] The Yukon Voyage, *The New York Post,* 18 August 1898

speed of five miles an hour.[30] The lake is not over five miles wide at any point, and often narrower. The shores are bold most of the way and banked by high hills which stretch along either side of the entire length of the lake and are covered with the soft green of fir and spruce timber. We were in the midst of a fleet of at least 250 boats, which remained insight all the way down, passing and repassing each other according to changes of the wind, and those who sailed fast enough to pass us were soon replaced by others from the rear. We ran up the Stars and Stripes soon after leaving Bennett, and many a cheer was raised along the shore and in boats near us. Several saw- mills on the bank saluted the flag with their whistles, and we always answered with three cheers.

It was like one long-continued yacht race all the way to Thirty-mile River, where it became very dangerous to sail very close to others. The water in all these lakes, Bennett, Tagish, Marsh and Lebarge, is of the clearest blue color and deep enough for navigation, except in very few places, such as the head Lakes Marsh and Tagish. We are drawing about 24 inches of water, and where we could go all could follow, as few required that much. Only twice did we meet any ice, and in both cases, we pushed through easily. The ice was soft and honeycombed, and it only required a line ashore and a few set poles at work to get through it. These ice fields might have been dangerous had the wind been blowing hard enough to put them in motion, but lying still as they were, a boat could be polled through without danger. Lebarge is by far the finest of this chain of lakes. It is five miles wide in some places and from the middle of the

---

[30] NWMP records at Lake Bennett, record of people entering the Yukon via boats:
May 19, 1898, LEVENGOOD, R OH- Scrow 184 & 2 small boats
May 19, 1898, LEVENGOOD, J OH- Scrow 184 & 2 small boats

lake on down there are many rocky islands and beautiful little bays. We could see trout and grayling jumping out of the water around these islands, but failed to catch any. Only one fish did we get all the way down and that was caught trolling through Bennett.

The Canadian mounted police have arranged a sort of registering system to keep track of this rush. They required us to register and take a number for our boat at Bennett, and then at four points on the way down we were called in to report.[31] These reporting stations were at Tagish House in Six-mile River, Big and little Salmon Rivers and Fort Selkirk. No questions are asked by the officers in charge except in regard to whisky. At Tagish House all boats are inspected, and as this requires some little time the shore was lined for three miles with boats waiting for the inspector's signature. Some had been waiting in line for two days and we expected to have to do the same, but the inspector caught sight of some beef hanging on our decks. He probably had not tasted fresh beef for some months, and was glad to inspect the Buckeye at once. We got away in a very short time, and he had beef that night for supper.

At the foot of Lake Marsh, we entered Lewes River. At its head the current is slow, but gradually grows swifter as we approach the canyon and White Horse Rapids. We reached a point about four miles above the canyon late Thursday night, and on Friday morning we dropped down to within a half mile of the mouth of the canyon. Here we tied up for a day to give our sailors an opportunity to look at the rapids. They never would have taken the chances on a Friday, anyway. We had some trouble in making this landing; our anchor— a couple of rocks tied in a wooden frame—broke, and we were drifting towards the canyon. We managed to get a line ashore and

---

[31] Pan for Gold Database, www.geneology.com

stop her after a moment of wild excitement. Four of us then started down to pick a channel and watch others make the run. The banks were lined with people, most of whom were interested in some boat, and as each party came down over the waves in the canyon they were cheered to the echo. All seemed to be making this part of the run safely, but just below the canyon, in Squaw Rapids, a half dozen boats of all sizes were piled up on a rock in the middle of the stream. They formed a very good but expensive channel stake for those coming after them. About two miles below the end of the canyon the river makes a sharp turn to the left, beyond which bend a field of white water marks the entrance to White Horse Rapids. Then comes another bend this time to the right; and from this point on through the narrows, a half mile below, where the river rushes through a gap 60 feet wide, there is no turning back—a boat once in must go through. The narrows are formed by two ledges of rock which project from the banks of the stream and a view of the rapids can be had from either of these ledges.

We stood there for several hours watching the boats shoot by us. It was a scene of continued excitement. Nearly all got through safely, but one scow struck on the rock about 200 yards above the gap. She had a crew of three men, and when she struck, the man at the bow-sweep was thrown out, and he came down through the gap swimming, with head and shoulders out of water. We stood within ten feet of him and saw him shoot by us and disappear beneath a great wave just at the end of the gap. He was probably caught by an undercurrent and dragged along the river bottom, for nothing was seen of him afterward. The scow was still tottering upon the rock above, and her crew, now reduced to two, were preparing to save themselves as best they could. One had tied two oars together and put them under his arm, while the other was taking down the mast, no doubt intending to swim through the gap. There was wild excitement on both shores of the river now, and men were --- up and down shouting to those in the scow to stay there till something could be done for them. Several started up the banks in search of boats in which they could drop down to the scow and save the two, while others went in search of lines. There was really nothing that could be done, for no boat could stop at that point in the rapids to take on passengers, and no man could throw a line from shore to the scow. The only chance for those two men was to cling to cling to their boat until she was washed off the rocks. The current would take them through the gap, and they could be picked up on the other side.

The scow was fast breaking up, and the water was pouring over her from end to end. When finally she swung around, her bottom was torn out, and, lightened by the escape of her cargo, she was washed clear of the rock and floated down through the gap, turning over and over and those two men clambering from side to side, now in the water and now out, but always clinging to the wreck. Beyond the gap by about 100 feet, the current forms an eddy and many a boat is drawn in here against the rocks. The wreck made a turn toward these rocks, went part way in, and was then caught by the current again and drifted further down. As she swung in towards shore one of her crew made a leap towards a small skiff lying in the eddy, missed it, and was carried out into the current and drowned. The last of the crew clung to his boat till he was picked off a mile below the rapids. Later that same day, another larger scow was wrecked on this same rock. She had a crew of old Klondikers, one of the Lippy, a mine owner of some distinction here. Lippy's wife and child were saved with the other passengers, but they all clung to their boat till taken off beyond the rapids.

That night a crew of eight was chosen to take the Buckeye through both canyon and rapids, and early the next morning everything was put in readiness to make the run, our mast lowered, cabin cleared away, and a bow-sweep put in. We arranged to land in an eddy just below the canyon and there unload part of our goods, as we were drawing a little too much water for the squaw rapids. I was a member of the scow's crew, but I can't tell you much about that trip—it was done so quickly. I remember the great towering walls of the canyon, the rush and combining of the water in the middle of the stream, and how the spray flew over the bow of our boat wetting the feet of the two men at the bow-sweep. We made the landing easily, unloaded about three tons of flour, and then put out into the stream again to shoot the rapids. We passed wrecks in squaw rapids and went through the shallow water there without touching once, kept the right hand channel in White Horse Rapids, and went through the gap without shipping so much as a bucket of water. I stood at one of the oars coming down, but had little rowing to do. A boat will go through all right without steering if she is properly started. Start to clear that rock where so many are wrecked and a boat will shoot straight for the gap, and if she is not sucked into the rapids there is no danger. I went through four times the next day and wore off some of the excitement of it. We made up a piloting crew of four and earned good wages there for one day, while the rest of the party made the portage from below the canyon down to the rapids.

There are two tramways running there now that carry goods around both canyon and rapids for one cent a pound. Each has built a roadbed, Hepburn on the left bank and Macauley on the right, and both are doing a good business. They are expecting a big rush in August and September—more even than they have now---and when the two lines of steamers commence running above and below the rapids, these tramways will no doubt form the connecting link between two great lines of transportation. Both tramways hire professional pilots for the canyon and the rapids and make large amounts. Twenty dollars is the usual rate for a small boat, while scows bring from $50 to $100, one pilot making as many as six trips per day. All boats land above the canyon, and nearly all owners are persuaded not to attempt the run without a pilot. Many of them could not be hired to go down in a boat even with a pilot, and are only too glad to pay the price demanded for pilotage. I saw one man who went through the canyon alone. He landed just above White Horse, and having been badly frightened by as much of the rapids as he had seen, determined to hire a pilot the next morning. He drove in a stake on the bank, tied up his boat, and went to bed. During the night his stake pulled out, and the current, catching him just right carried him down all safe and sound. He woke up just before reaching the gap, and all he could do was to tuck his head under the covers and let her go. It saved him the pilotage charge if it did scare him.

Thirty-three miles below the rapids we enter Lake Labarge, and from its end down it is all a river voyage---simply drifting with the current and watching for rocks and bars. Thirty-mile River, the outlet of Labarge, is the worst piece of water in the entire trip. The current is very swift and dangerous rocks abound all through. It requires the utmost vigilance to keep clear of them, and many boats have been wrecked here. We came down just after a jam had occurred, in which four parties had lost boats and outfits. We had several narrow escapes in Thirty-mile River, and in one case a log that had been thrown on to a rock and stuck there was all that saved us from destruction. The only thing that bothered us was the mosquitoes, and they are all that they have been represented.

I have seen little of this great log cabin city as yet. I walked through it once on Sunday, when everything was closed; saw hotels where dinner was offered at $2.50; stores where eggs sold at $3 per dozen and apples higher still. There were men in swarms on every corner and on all the streets. The majority had the air of waiting for something to turn up, and the few who did not looked as though they had already reaped the harvest of several turns. We are to stop here for a number of days, more for information than to prospect. About half the boys have gone out to the mines to learn what they can. We may of course decide to stay here. Advice is freely given and is about equally favorable to American territory and the Klondike region. The miner is better protected in Alaska than he is here, but of course if there are better fields in this territory than beyond the line, here we should stay. Two steamers which were frozen in near Circle City last fall have just landed here with a small cargo. None has come up from St. Michaels yet, so no mail has arrived by that route; but a scow came down the river this afternoon bringing some thirty bags of letters, which will be distributed in a few days. This letter will go out tomorrow by Canadian mounted police, but I doubt if it reaches you before the 1st of August.

H.R.Huntington

The latest news from the Sandusky-Klondike party has just been received by Mrs. Livengood of Sand Hill. *The Sandusky Daily Register*, August 13, 1898:[32]

Dawson,   June 12

Well mother, I will now give you a description of our trip to Dawson. We left Bennett City May 20, at 2 p.m. and ran all night. We went as far as a place called Caribou Crossing, stayed there until noon and then started again, passed around Windy Arm and then broke through a field of ice into Lake Taglan and sailed all night and landed at the customs house at 9:30 a.m. We got our papers and left again at 3 p.m.

There must have been 1,000 or more waiting for their clearance papers and some of them had been there a day. Well, we sailed until we went to a field of ice, anchored and stayed all night and at 12 started for the field of ice and broke our way across it and sailed all night, and at 9 a.m. we went into Thirty Mile River and went as far as Mile's canyon and tied up. On June 4 we shot the White Horse rapids all right. The crew was composed of Captain Snevely, Miller, Huntington, Minzer, Shay and a man named Hauland and myself. We went like a rifle ball for three miles and we made it in about ten minutes.

---

[32] Fortune Hunters in Alaska Wilds, *Sandusky Daily Register,* 13 August 1898

Smith, Miller and Howard have been shooting the rapids all day. They made about 100 miles today. Left White Horse and are sailing down Thirty Mile River. Struck Lake Labarge at 4:30 p.m. and sailed all night and at 1:07 this morning in a bad river on account of stone and swift water, but got through all right.

June 8---
Sailing down the Lewes River at 12, tied up on account of bad winds. Broke two oars and had to make some new ones.

June 9---
Started at three this morning, went through the Five Fingers rapids, landed at Fort Selkirk at 8 p.m. and tied up for the night. Tried to make some wood but the mosquitoes were so bad that we started again and went down about four miles and tied up. There we had a good nights rest.

June   11
Started at 4a.m. Everything went well until we landed on a sand bar good and proper. It took five hours to get off but we did it just the same.

I have been talking to Willie Bruce. He has been in Dawson for six weeks. He looks as he did as a boy, and said he was never more pleased to meet any one party than he was the Sandusky boys. He is putting up a log cabin now and will soon be in the butcher business. He told me he bought two moose and cleared $300 Gold is plentiful here and so are the people. Well, will say goodbye to all. Hoping to hear from all soon.

JAY

The following letter was received by the family of George J. Miller from that hustling member of the Sandusky-Klondike party and contains some good things for his friends to read.[33]

Lewes River N.W.T.   June 12, 1898

We have passed Hooto Linoux and Big Salmon River and it will take but two or three hours today to reach Dawson City. I got up out of bed at 4 this morning and worked up to breakfast time.

I hope you received my letters, you and George last week. I could not get them off on account of having no postage stamps from Canada and could not buy any for love or money. They ran out of them at the post office.

We shot the rapids at Miles Canyon and White Horse rapids and also Square rapids, and as they all come in rotation, it is a quick ride. Going through the White Horse Rapids, it is three-quarters of a mile long and it was done in about three-quarters of a minute. Jim Anderson and myself handled the stern oar and Chas Smith and Jay Livengood steered with the bow oar. Howard Huntington, Judge Shay and Abe Minzer handled. Capt. Snevely was also on deck. I forgot to mention him at first. We are lying alongside the bank about one mile below Little Salmon River at 6 o'clock.

On thirty miles of Lewes River we had lots of rocks, bars and rapids to contend with, but up to now we have had no mishaps. By tomorrow morning we will shoot the five fingers rapids and then the Rink rapids.

---

[33] George J. Miller Writes, *The Sandusky Daily Register,* 18 August 1898

There were two people drowned in the White Horse rapids last Friday. Lots of fellows lost everything they had by the rocks in the river's rapids. We have been very careful in following up the streams and our scow is a good one. Captain Snevely's ideas must have been running wild about boats. In the start it was to be four boats and now it's down to one, the Buckeye.

We are going to prospect as soon as we strike Dawson in parties of three. Howard Huntington, myself and Cowan from Milan will go together. I am well pleased with the choice, although we had planned otherwise. Howard can try his hand at frying flapjacks or pancakes made of flour and cornmeal mixed with water. We will also have turkey—that is if we shoot one or find one to shoot. Our turkey now is bacon stuffed with grease, and bread as a side dish. We also have ice cream minus the ice and the cream. Rolled oats and adulterated milk passes as the cream and ice.

We still have some of Buck (one of our oxen) left. Berry is all eaten up, except about a quarter, which we jerked. The rest we will jerk with our teeth after it is cooked. I suppose you know what jerked meat is; if not I will tell you. It is cut in strings, salted and hung up in the sun to dry, and you eat that when you are tramping as it is, or you can cook it too if you wish.

Everything around here is green and wildflowers are growing here by the acre. Some are very small flowers which are real beauties and have a sweet odor to them. I hope that George is doing well and will try and work hard to make something for us.

GEORGE J. MILLER

The Creeks

The valleys of the Klondike watershed were no different than the thousands of others that made up the Yukon Plateau. Like so much of the North, there was not enough moisture in the Yukon interior to support an ice age, thus they were untouched by any glacial advance. These deep, mile wide valleys were terraced by benches that suggested ancient upheavals in the earth's crust. Far below, blue-white creeks meandered over the chalky gravels.

There was no 'mother lode' in the Klondike, no thick vein of hard rock gold in the bowels of some dome or hill. That had long since been ground into nuggets and dust by the same force that formed the valleys. "Moose pastures", they were called by the prospectors.

Far below the floors of these pastures and high up on the benches, caught in the flakey bedrock of subterranean stream beds, long since gone dry, lay the richest gravels in the world. To find those ancient streambeds or the "pay streaks" as they were called, one must dig a shaft down thirty feet or more through frozen ground. The gold was in a layer 2-3 feet thick directly over the bedrock and had to be brought to the surface in buckets. The gold was then washed out when water was available in the spring, using a sluice and a gold pan. Only now did the late arrivals comprehend the effort required to dig out the gold. Many had thought of digging for gold in terms of digging for potatoes.

As often happens when a gold strike is made, the original claim is not the richest. The work was centered at the juncture of Bonanza and Eldorado, not far from the original discovery claim. Eldorado was the richest creek in the Klondike with at least 30 claims worth, at approximately a million dollars each. High above the confluence of the two creeks were three gold laden benches: French Hill, Cheechako Hill, and Gold Hill. In whose depths the famous 'White Channel", an ancient alluvial stream bed snaked and twisted, loaded with gold dust. The valley between French Hill and Cheechako Hill was called "Big Skookum Gulch", and at its mouth, the richest single sliver in history, lay the famous Dick Lowe Fraction. The fraction was a pie shaped wedge of land just 86 feet wide at its broadest point, accidentally created by imperfect staking. It was reluctantly claimed by an ex-muleskinner who took a half million from it.[34]

Mr. A.A. Hill who was the accompanying correspondent for The Sandusky Daily Register newspaper described Dawson City:

"We are in the greatest mining camp in the world. Individuals may have given false colors to the picture, too bright, too somber, --- but the yellow metal is everywhere. It is practically in every medium of exchange, and it is the cheapest thing in town. More dust bags are in evidence than pocket handkerchiefs and nothing sells for less than 50 cents. These are the first observations to greet the visiting stranger, and the next is the domination of whisky and gambling. The banks, the newspaper offices, the post office and the churches are mostly standing on side streets. But the whisky bar, the dance hall and the gambling room are in the forefront of the business center. There are some half dozen places where faro, roulette, poker and keno are being played night and day."[35]

---

[34] Pierre Burton, The Klondike Quest, *Boston Mills Press*, 1983, 1987
[35] A.A. Hill, Correspondent, *Sandusky Daily Register,* 1898

The ACM Co. was a late arrival to the creeks of Dawson. Like other latecomers, they experienced the disappointment of finding the richest claims already taken. Despite their late arrival they were not discouraged, and they decided to search farther upstream on Bonanza Creek, hoping to find a good prospect. They registered several claims that might prove to be successful in the future. They soon found that high taxes and the rules and regulations concerning mining claims in Canada were so restricting that their chances of any success would be severely limited. After discussing the situation in Dawson, Captain Snevely decided to leave six of his miners at Dawson to prove up their claims, and he would take the rest of the men down the Yukon River to American territory where regulations were not so stifling.

Ross and Jay Livengood, Perry Hutchins, Henry Zurcher and Julian Shay stayed behind in Dawson to prospect for any claims that might have been missed and to test the value of the claims they had hastily made upon arrival. It would be three months before they would rejoin the main party at Eagle.

Although the Company's claims in Canadian territory later proved to be of little value the time Ross spent in Dawson produced some of his richest memories.

While in Dawson, the men, always attracted to places where music was being played, visited the barrooms and saloons where they saw performances by the illustrious "Klondike Kate" and recognized Jack London, the author of "Call of the Wild" among the patrons. Ross claimed that "Jack was a booze fighter who drank everything in sight."[36] Ross savored his memories of the times he spent in the saloons of Dawson as he recalled the conversations and tales told by the miners in those barrooms so many years ago. Many of Ross's stories resembled scenes from the books of Jack London as he recalled the miners betting on their dog's ability to pull heavily loaded sleds. One of his recollections described a time when the men killed a bear that had a cub. Knowing that the cub would starve if they left it behind, they decided to put it on a leash and bring it back to camp. The camp's dogs seeing a bear in the camp rushed to attack. "The little feller's paws were powerful and as quick as lightning." Ross recalled, "The cub would spin around and cuff a dog nipping at its flank sending it tumbling head over heels and yipping back to where it had come from. The dogs soon lost interest in the cub."[37]

From THE KLONDIKE NUGGET

Dawson, Alaska   JUNE 16, 1898

Ross Livengood, Perry Hutchins, H.W. Zurcher and Julian L. Shay, of the Sandusky party of 20 who recently arrived, made a discovery on 70 below on Bonanza and brought their clean up into the city Monday evening. Two hundred and fifty pounds of bear

---

[36] It is unlikely that anyone in Ross' party actually saw Lack London since he left home on June 8, 1898, which was four days before the Sandusky party arrived. (Franklin Walker, "Jack London & the Klondike", Huntington Library, p.167)

[37] From remembrances of tales told to the author by his grandfather in the 1940's

meat at $1.25 per pound is not a bad day's work. The honor of the discovery belongs to Mr. Livengood.

The above story was clipped from a copy of the Klondike Nugget sent to Gust Zurcher of this city by his brother Henry who went to Alaska with the Sandusky party. In a letter accompanying the paper were four nuggets ranging from the size of a pea to that of a bean, and it was when the party were returning from the search for these nuggets that the bear was found. As the "Nugget" says, it was not a bad day's work.[38]

James Sanderson described the hunt in a letter to his wife from Dawson City:

DAWSON City, N.W.T.   June 19, 1898

Last Monday night four of the boys started up the Klondike to take a look at the mines. When about six miles from Dawson they run onto a large brown bear. Ross Livengood had his rifle, and they immediately gave chase to bruin up the mountain, with Henry Zurcher a close second with an axe. Ross fired seven shots and hit him every time. After the sixth shot Mr. bear stopped and raised himself on his hind legs, when Ross put a ball through his head, which tumbled him 75 to 100 feet down the mountain to the trail below, where Judge Shay and Perry Hutchins had selected their tree.

They lashed him to two poles and brought him to the boat, arriving about 3:30 am. He weighed 110 pounds and the boys got

---

[38] From The Klondike, *The Norwalk Daily Reflector,* 27 July 1898

$110 for him. We used the head and kept the skin, which is worth $25 more.[39]

Mrs. Livengood had received the following letter from her son Jay and kindly permitted its publication in the Register that all the friends of the Sandusky-Klondikers may know what the boys were doing in that faraway land of gold. In it the writer tells about Alaska and the operations and intentions of our gold-seekers.[40]

On Eldorado Creek,   June 24.1898
Dear Mother:

This is a pleasant morning and our little band if six is as happy as can be under the circumstances. We have been packing some of our goods 16 miles up the river and I want to say to you that when one has a pack on his back and travels over this trail he will know what hard work is it is up one hill and down the other and through marshy places. The hillside is covered with mud and water, and it isn't a very inviting trip to make every day for five or six days, but still it has to be done. Today will be the last trip for a few days. Ross and myself will make it and get the mail.

Some of the boys are going up the river to prospect on some bench claims you can see people washing up gold in any direction you look. The river is staked for 100 miles, so you see it isn't as much fun as might be supposed.

---

[39] The Land of Gold, *The Sandusky Star,* 28 July 1898
[40] Nearly Everything Taken, *The Sandusky Daily Register,* 30 July 1898

We are talking of going beyond any other prospector, where the white man's foot has never trod and see what we can find. We will make relay stations for we could not carry enough to make the trip. We would not want to come right back and traveling 100 miles in this country is something altogether different than in Ohio. Although this is a very pretty country in the summer it is very hard to travel through. There are all kinds of wildflowers growing out here and lots that are very pretty. The hillsides are covered with them; of every hue, though one would not think that all of our eastern songbirds would be found in a cold country like this where the ground is frozen as far down as any man has dug---one dug down 96 feet and it was frozen to the bottom. You can turn the moss over anywhere and find the ground frozen. It is even frozen under the rivers. There is all kinds of game to be found here, moose elk and caribou, bear of all kinds, sheep and goats and wolves. Moose beef is worth $2 per pound. A man brought one to Dawson the other day and got $1,000 for it. He made it in three days hunting.

When I was back in the states the people told me that I would never see lightning out here nor hear thunder, but that is a mistake, for during the last three days it has been thundering and raining. It is light all the time now and if it should remain cloudy for three or four days you could not distinguish night from day. The birds sing all the time; both night and day and you never see the stars in this part of the world.

Well, I don't know or can't think of anything to write about at this time. It looks very much like rain and Ross and I have a 16 mile walk to make and carry a pack back 16 miles to map again, and when we get back and get a flapjack and a slice of bacon and a cup of coffee beneath our belts we will feel better and about the next move will to string up our beds, shake up the feathers and move a few of the stones that were punching us in the back the night before.

When you get everything ready you jump in and go to sleep---if you can. About the time you think you are going to sleep you will find a million and one mosquitoes drilling holes in your anatomy. I have my hair clipped and maybe the mosquito doesn't get in his work on my head! Well, Mother, I will write you a little more when I get to Dawson.

June 26

Ross and I started from camp last night at 9:30 and got to our cache at 2:30. Our cache is located at Lewistown, just across from Dawson. The Klondike River separates the two towns. They are nearly the same size, and both are doing a rushing business. Just below Dawson is an encampment of about 500 Indians: some of them speak the English language and are neat and clean. Lots of the squaws dress in silks, wear "foxy" hats and kid gloves and one would hardly expect to find so much style in a frozen wilderness amongst a band of savages.

You ought to see the people trying to have gardens out here. You would see a little patch of ground planted to garden seeds. I saw a good many planted on top of cabins, but garden truck doesn't do well here for the days are too warm and the nights too cold. It freezes a little every night and that is the reason gold has been scattered all over the country.

Ross has just got breakfast and I must quit writing and eat my meal. The bill of fare is bacon, oatmeal, flapjacks, eggs coffee and milk.

It has commenced to rain, and I guess we are elected to stay here all day. Ross has laid down to take a nap for he knows what 16 miles with a pack on his back means in this country. Last night when coming down I picked a few wildflowers to send you. I don't know to what shape they will reach you but will send them just the same. This would be a great country for Rush, it would keep him guessing to name all the flowers that grow in it. Tell Biglow this is just the place for him, he could go out in the hills and get all kinds of game and a good price for all he could kill.

From your son,

Jay Livengood

Eagle City

Captain J.E. Snevely at the head of the Sandusky-Klondike party, and the Register's correspondent writes the following letter.[41]

Eagle City, Alaska,   June 29

Our party is now landed at Eagle City. We stopped at Dawson City ten days, hustled around and got 12 bench claims and left six men with three months provisions to prospect there. Eagle City, where the balance of our party is located, is at the mouth of Mission creek, about ten miles down the Yukon from the boundary line and has heretofore been given on the maps as Belle Isle. American creek comes into Mission creek about a half mile above the mouth. Forty Mile, Seventy Mile, Mission and Birch creeks all lead up in a region about ten miles north of this point, and all old timers tell us that this head waters country is easier of access from this point than from any other on the river.

This, together with the fact that very rich discoveries have recently been made on Seventy Mile and Mission creeks, has drawn a great many people from Circle City and Dawson and quite a town boom is on here.

We got in just in time to get 12 of the best and most desirable business lots on the waterfront. Our predecessors had been looking for high ground and took such as showed high on the bank, but we

---

[41] Gold Prospects Rich In Promise, *The Sandusky Daily Register,* 2 August 1898

got what the transportation companies and the people both wanted, and at first thought could not be gotten together.

They both selected their sites when the water was way up and out of the river. Now when it is down to its normal stage the transportation companies are on a flat bar and the people on a high bank, and all about a mile apart.

When we came in, we stopped just below the transportation company's location and found deep water, a good landing and vacant lots.

We at once took up the lots and cleared them of underbrush, and the people now all say, "Why you have the best lots in the whole business." The land is level for a half mile back and is covered with bunch grass, which would make fine pasture for stock for about four months in the year. I am greatly surprised at the climate here, and the growth of vegetation. You would never suspect that you were in 65 north latitude.

Some of the old timers like the climate so well here that they prefer to stay here to going out. I find that the only way to get back into this country is to establish relay stations every 30 to 40 miles.

We will build here a good substantial log storehouse, then 30 or 40 miles out another, and so on until we reach out about 200 miles or more.

Four of the boys here are out prospecting, while ten of us are clearing ground and building a house.

The stories about mosquitoes have not been exaggerated much. It is almost impossible to get any rest from them, but it has been proven at Dawson that by clearing up and draining they disappear.

I am keeping myself well smoked while I am writing.

I met an old friend, a boyhood playmate, who has discovered, and now owns the wonderfully rich bench claim on French Gulch Hill, tributary to Eldorado, where each man everyday washes out $1,000 with a rocker.

We have ten claims on Eldorado below and on the opposite side from his rich mine.

Mr. Anderson, an old-timer, and myself, are going out in a few days to look up some forfeited claims on American creek, and since we are here we found that American creek is just as good as Bonanza on the Klondike and the laws are so much better.

The Canadian laws are even worse than we thought before we left home.

We have a post office established here and will get our first-class mail matter via Dyea every two weeks. All other mail will come via St. Michael's whenever it can get here.

Day before yesterday the first boat, the Hampton, went down the river. Yesterday morning the P.B. Weare went down with four tons of gold dust aboard.

This morning the Bella went down, but as the Hamilton and Bella did not stop here, we cannot tell how much treasure they took out. This, however, will not be news when you get it. The Seattle No. 1 is the first of all the boats that started up last fall to get up this far.

She went up the 22nd, the day we came in here. All hands are well and working.

J.E.SNEVELY

George Miller, who is with the Sandusky party of Klondikers, writes the following letter:[42]

Eagle City, Ala.,   July 1,'98.

Rosa C. Miller,   Sandusky, O.

Dear Wife,

I received two letters at Dawson from you and George, after laying there for a week. I sent you letters every week and I hope you received them all. You need not send any papers because they won't handle them out here, but if there is anything of importance in the paper cut it out and send it. Tell Mr. Bang not to send any more. I don't know why they accept papers at the post office for Alaska when they don't carry them into the interior.

Tell Slate I received his letter long after I sent one to him. It is a hard matter to get mail out here; they keep it in the office for months before they try to distribute it. I have seen men get letters out of the Dawson office that had lain there for over a year.

We went out prospecting, that is Howard Huntington, Cowan and myself, and staked 13 claims on Last Chance creek and we look now

---

[42] At Eagle City, *The Sandusky Star Journal,* 18 August 1898

as though we had been out fighting Spaniards and that they peppered us with bird shot "all mosquito bites." I used to think I had seen mosquitoes, but I found out my mistake when here I walked through water and brush and moss very near two feet thick. I tell you it was a tough proposition; it was the hardest walking of all in the moss; you would have to pick your feet for keeps if you wanted to get over it or you would get tangled in it. Howard Huntington calls the brush the jungles and the only thing missing therein are the animals such as lions, tigers and panthers, but we see bears and moose and more than enough of the before mentioned mosquitoes. If I have seen millions of mosquitoes in the states, I have seen here in the last eight days a million for each one seen there. I had a notion of clinching their bills when they drove them through the blanket, but on second thought I changed my mind for fear they would fly away with my blanket leaving me exposed to their bills and I don't like to be billed like that, not by a long bill.

We are now about 10 miles across the lines the N.W. territory. Eagle City is 112 miles from Dawson City. Tuesday and Wednesday of this week we had heavy thundershowers. On Tuesday it was on the mountain and we thought it was a landslide, but later on we found out it was thunder, and the next evening got it accompanied with rain and hail and it kept up for quite a while. We returned to the scow last night at 10 O'clock and were pretty hungry. We have 12 town lots laid out here. Dell Deyo is recorder of Eagle City. He was elected after being here two days. There was some dissatisfaction with the other recorder, and they bounced him. They keep a man in office until they get tired, and then they give him the g.b. They took the mast out of our scow and planted it before our tent, or rather the recorder's office and old glory floats in the breeze.

Deacon Widman has gone up the river with Theim, Fettle, Zurcher and Hutchins to cut logs for our cabins in Eagle City. I believe they are going to build two of them. We have a nice view of the mountains from our camping place. Everything looks so fresh and green just like "we Klondikers green." Well, we are past being called tenderfeet. I believe that some of us could walk on carpet tacks by this time.

Yesterday forenoon as I was coming down Last Chance with three beds, filled with clothing and shoes, on my back, I happened to step in a hole and both feet slid out from under me, and I lay stretched at full length in the cool ice water and my bundle went on the bank without a drop of water on it. I called for Howard to pull the bundle away before it would roll into the water, as I kept on sliding, but the call was unnecessary, the bundle was safe where it was. The bundle was very light and very bulky, and you ought to have seen me crawling under the bushes and logs across the creek and between trees, and I was sure to get caught by a dry tree and have the bundle jerked off of my back or I would have to twist myself around a half dozen times to get out of the difficulty.

At times my foot would get caught and I would be thrown forward on my face and I would have to look around for my bundle. If Howard Huntington could have caught a snapshot of me, he could have sold the pictures to some comic paper. I have sent two letters to Albert Bergmoser and two to Cowan. I hope they have received them.

All claims on different creeks are taken up. Six of our boys are working twelve of them at Bonanza and Eldorado creeks.

Our flags attract a great deal of attention and many a cheer was given the scow Buckeye with the flags floating overhead. But the flags are on the scow no longer but wave over Uncle Sam's soil.

Spenser wrote me and said if I would send him an Esquimaux he would send me a Spaniard when he gets to go to war. Tell him I will send him the first one I can capture, or better still, I will send a papoose if I can get some squaw to donate one.

This morning a sudden squall came up and down came our tent, but it was only a puff of wind and all over in a short time as if nothing had happened. One of the men's hats blew off and went straight up in the air as high as our flagpole and then dropped down right at the foot of it.

Captain Snevely started out prospecting this morning taking with him Sanderson, Koegle, Shay and one or two others. There are quite a number of fellows from different states that are getting homesick and are selling out.

Dell Deyo has a double job cooking and entertaining visitors. We, of course, wish to swell our town or Louse will get ahead of us and every lot is a fiver for our company.

I forgot to mention that when we went out prospecting, we could have caught a lot of game if we would have left our frying pan and shovels at home. They make a lot of noise when they come in contact with trees and scare the game. If I went with a party of Sanduskians and we carried anything of that nature along with us all we could find would be the tracks of the animals.

We had some fun staking claims, staking five as we were going up the mountains only to come across claims with the very same numbers as our own, then we had to retrace our steps and chop the names off again from the trees. We did that three or four times, then we followed up the mountains and found it staked all the way. We must have walked 25 miles and gained nothing upon the creek, but we found several below Discovery claim and staked them. We dug down about 10 or 12 feet only to have it cave in on us; then we packed our goods on board the scow and went to headquarters.

Cowan has long legs for so small a man and keeps up with Huntington admirably but I, although somewhat taller than Cowan, have smaller legs than he and it keeps me hustling to keep up with them.

I don't know why I don't get more letters, as I have written to several men about town but have received no replies. But I expect they don't like the nonsense I write.

I believe they call the Indians Alientes or some such name. They catch trout, white grayling, suckers and pike in the river but I have not seen many fish up here, but I have been told there will be plenty of all kinds in August and that may give me a chance for some tall yarns.

Well, I must close as I have no more news, give my best to Kate, Albert and Lydia. Tell Spencer to send those red-hot decoys to Sanderson and Koegle. Well, goodbye. My love to yourself, George and Grace.

I remain your husband,

George

The following news from the Sandusky-Klondike party was received by Mrs. Livengood of Sand Hill from her son Jay, who is a member of the party. The second letter was received a day or two before and is also very interesting, being descriptive of the trip to Dawson.[43]

Dawson City   July 10.

I thought I would write and tell you how we are getting along We are all right and feeling good. Ross and I just got back from a long trip over the mountains. I have been up to Flat creek a distance of 65 miles. It was quite a trip. Started the night of June 27th and got back July 8. We ran out of provisions and had to come back. We had nothing to eat from the time we started until we got in camp. It was quite a walk---65 miles---and it rained nearly all the time, which made it very unpleasant for us, not saying anything about the mosquitoes, which are as thick as a swarm of bees---they don't do a thing but alight on you, stand on their heads, and drive their bills into you up to their eyes. Oh, but they are warm birds!

I tell you it is a sight when one is on top of the dome of the divide to look over the country. It looks like a hay field all bunched up to haul in. Just one mass of small mountains and you can see the Rockies. They run in one great long chain, but the others are all over and you cannot find an acre of ground that hasn't got a mountain on it.

We are going to build a boat to go up the river in. It will be 25 feet long, 18 inches wide on the bottom and three feet on top. Then we

---

[43] Over Whitehorse Rapids, *Sandusky Daily Register,* 13 August 1898

will go up the Klondike to Flat Creek to prospect. We have to build it in order to take provisions to last while we are prospecting. We have struck a nice country and it has never been prospected yet. There is lots of game there to and when I get back will write and tell you what we find. Will be back in two or three weeks. There has been a rush up on Dominion creek. About 500 joined the rush---woman and men. I saw woman with their packs on their backs going alone, sometimes on the run, for all they were worth. The distance is 50 miles.

How did you all spend the fourth? In Dawson they had a big time. Ross and I were prospecting. It rained all day and we got good and wet. We were out all day and night without anything to eat. Ross shot a duck and when we got on Flat Creek, we cooked our duck and made some flapjacks and had a good meal. It is something you don't get every day---flapjacks and duck---in this country. While you folks were drinking warm water, we were drinking ice water and when it gets too warm we can climb to the top of a mountain and sit in the snow, so you see you haven't got the best of us so very much after all. Still we have no Cedar Point or Johnson's Island, but lots of mountains. When Ross and I were on top of the dome the sun was going down and when we got on the other side it was coming up. It seemed to just dodge behind a high point of the Rockies and come out on the other side. If you lie down and go to sleep up here when you wake up, you cannot tell whether it is day or night. Ross and I lost one day on our trip. You can have a watch, compass and calendar, and if someone would ask you what the day of the week was you could not tell, for I asked a dozen whether it was Saturday or Sunday and they all said Sunday, and when I got to Dawson I found out it was Saturday

We haven't heard from the boys down in American territory. The mail came in yesterday but won't be distributed for three or four days and perhaps we will get a letter from them, then.

I hope I get one from Ohio. I did not wait to see if there was one for me, but if I do get one will mail another right away. It is noon and I cannot think of anything to write about, for Abe is getting dinner and dinner is uppermost in my mind now and my stomach won't let me forget it, so with love to you all I will close this scrawl.

Your son.

JAY

J.E. Snevely writes:

Eagle City, Alaska   July 13

(Special Correspondence)----We are still at Eagle City and will make this our permanent headquarters.

We have our first little misfortune to report. My grip was stolen yesterday while I was away up the river opening up our 160-acre claim. It happened while Deyo, Huntington and Gleckner, who were left in camp, were eating dinner.

It contained my letter of credit, a lot of stamps, and a small amount of money in gold and silver as also some gold dust, a set of drawing instruments, a $25 compass, recording receipts, etc.

The loss is not heavy only the inconvenience and getting of duplicates of receipts. Have stopped payment on letter of credit and we have a good clue and expect to make the fellows cough up

The 160-acre claim I mention above is one we have lately secured. We have a never-failing spring on it that boils out of the surface of the earth about 50 feet above the level of the river and about 150 yards back of the bank. There is about three and a half feet of waste gravel on the bed rock and over it a foot of muck and moss which has to be removed to get at the pay dirt, which we feel quite sure will go three ounces or more to the shovel.

The bed rock slopes gently toward the river so that the tail of our sluice box will dump into the river. The spring affords an extra-large sluice head---that is a stream say solid six by 12 inches and it has sufficient pitch or fall to the river so it will carry through any sized rocks.

The gravel shows gold everywhere, not as coarse as American Gulch and not as fine as some we have worked. We will use quicksilver so none of the fine dust will get away. The water is so situated that we can sluice the whole 100 acres. The gravel is not frozen so that it is entirely summer diggings and can be worked five months of the year, as the water does not freeze up as early as if it were creek water.

In a week we will begin shoveling into the sluice boxes and have every reason to think we have a big thing. I think $50,000 a very low estimate of its value.

I do not know what the boys at Dawson are doing, but I think we have a big thing here if we do not get any more, but there are great opportunities here.

Besides our 160-acre claim we have 18 good town lots, eight claims on Last Chance creek and 12 claims at Dawson, so for the short time we have been here we have done well.

The boys will be down this week with two rafts of 100 logs each for houses and lumber. We will have comfortable winter quarters. We will put in the winter-on-winter diggings. Of course, there is plenty of work connected with it and it is not all fun but we are glad to report that with us the good much outweighs the bad.

We are all well and hope within a short time to report pleasing news.[44]

J.E. SNEVELY

The very entertaining letter published below, replete with good humor and good news was written by Dell Deyo, better known as "Klondike Dell" to Ed Knopf, one of his friends and old time chums in this city, and was eagerly read by everybody who was interested in the Sandusky-Klondike party---and who in this city was not interested?[45]

---

[44] The Boys Expect, *Sandusky Daily Register,* 3 September 1898
[45] "Klondike Dell" Sends a Letter, *Sandusky Daily Register,* 6 October 1898

Eagle City, Alaska, U.S.A.,   July 20

Ed. Kuopf, Sandusky, Ohio

Dear Friend Ed:

Mr. Shepherd of Toledo is here near us and we have become well acquainted, and he has kindly offered to take letters for all of us and to deliver them in person to any one in Sandusky, and he is going out in a few days; so I concluded it was a good chance to send you a letter, knowing it would be sure to reach you. The facilities for handling the mail are very poor here.

Well, I presume you Sandusky boys are having a gay time at Cedar Point; you and John and DeWitt especially; while we are amusing ourselves fighting "skeeters." I wrote John some time ago but as yet have received no answer but it does not follow that he has not written, for I have heard from no one for over two months. We are all well, and I have not been as well for many a day. I have been cooking as of late for all that are here, and I tell you it is a great picnic. I started out Sunday night at 9 o'clock to go about ten miles to take up a mining claim of 20 acres, and it took us about one and a half hours to get on top of the mountain, and after we got up there our guide got lost and we went many miles out of our way, and arrived at our destination at 3 o'clock Monday afternoon, tired hungry and footsore. Everyone travels at night here because it's cooler, and the "skeeters" are not so bad, and it is almost as light here at night as it is in the daytime, and then it is very warm here some days---100 in the shade---and yet you only have a few inches down to the frost, and that is frozen the Lord only knows how deep, and it is kept in that state by the heavy coat of moss, and it is worse than a feather bed to walk on.

Well Ed, while I have had some hard work to do, and made some long journeys, yet I would not take a great deal for the experience I have had and the wonderful sights I have seen. It is grand to be up on top of one of these mountains and see the sun rise and set, the different mountains and rivers in all directions. The birds are singing every hour of the night, and wildflowers of every description grow here everywhere and look the same as flowers one sees cultivated there. Wild gooseberries, currents, peas, rhubarb, huckleberries, dewberries all grow here and onions also, and if it was not for the pesky "skeeters' this would be a grand place to live, for the weather is very fine and healthy, with very little rain or wind. In fact, we have had only one good rain here this summer and then it rained nearly all day, and I was out in it all day, and felt none the worse for it. We would be glad to have it blow a little more, for then we are not troubled by the "skeeters." Today they are not bothering us, and I am glad of it, for I traveled all night and reached home at 4 a.m. and I will rest up and start out again tomorrow evening with grub enough on my back to last me until August 1st.

We built our boat at Bennett City at the head of Lake Bennett and started from there on May 30 and had a lovely trip over the lakes and rivers, the most exciting time being at the canyon, and White Horse rapids, where men were wrecked by the score nearly every day, and quite a few were drowned, in sight of men and woman and children---mostly men. But we came through in fine style and reached Dawson City all O.K., and found thousands were there ahead of us and nearly all disgusted with everything and everybody and found everything claimed for miles around. But most of these are men expecting to pick up nuggets any and everywhere.

We were not so easily discouraged and by a little work got on the inside and secured 12 claims on Eldorado and Bonanza Creeks, and those are the two last creeks in the Klondike district. We have left six of our men there to operate them and get more if possible, but the laws there are simply rotten, and unless there is a change Dawson will soon be dead. But there is no use talking, there are some very rich mines there, and there has been several millions gotten out from them this season. I have seen the gold sacks piled up like stove wood in some of the stores there, and the only money is dust, and you ought to be here if you want to see gambling. It is carried out on a large scale. One saloon took in $10,000 the first 24 hours they were open, and there are very few decent women in Dawson, and the dancing houses are doing a thriving business. Each dance only costs $2--$1 for the dance and $1 for a drink for you and the girl, but as I don't dance, drink, or smoke or have anything to do with woman, I got through very cheap. I have spent less than $2 all told since I left Seattle, March 13th; so you see I did not come here to spend money, but to make it if possible.

Well, 14 of us came here almost the last of June and landed by accident our boat in front of the recorders tent, and strange to say, we found 12 vacant lots on the water front and we immediately took them up, and there was a meeting called for that next night as the present recorder was going to resign, and before I knew what was going on, some of our boys had everything arraigned to have me elected recorder and then came to see and request me to accept, and I was unanimously elected, and then they all go for me for gobbling up the only office in town, only having been in the country and city about 48 hours. I have to acknowledge it was a little swift.

We now have 15 good sized lots here and have logs enough to build a good large log house, and are going at it right away so you see we are going to be comfortable this winter, and the boat landing is almost in front of our lots, and I really believe this is going to be a better town than Dawson, and that very soon, for it is a much nicer town site, and is in God's country. We have the largest flag here and as people come down the river they nearly all give us a salute, for the boat, "The Buckeye" with her crew of 20 men are known all along the route. This is centrally located for the whole gold belt of Alaska, and if there are any good discoveries made here there will be a regular stampede for here. In fact, the first three blocks back from the river and one mile along the river is all taken now, and I am recording and making transfers every day.

Besides our town property here, we have taken up six 20-acre mining claims on different creeks, and Howard Huntington and I took up two claims yesterday in the same territory, where they are now taking out nearly $75 per day for each man, shoveling, and besides we have one claim that consists of 160 acres and we control the whole and have named it the Lake Erie Mining district, and the creek we have named Buckeye. Everything is named after something or someone in the state.

The boys are all in a tent near here and I can hear them sing. Really and truly I have never felt homesick or had the blues since I started. I feel confident we are going to meet with success before we leave here. We had only been here a few days when a boat landed with two brothers and one sister, and one lady friend, all nice people from Seattle. The girls are both from Seattle and are school teachers, and are fine girls, and they came to see a Platt of the city, and I sat down on a log and one of them sat down on each side of me, and really, it had been so long since I had been in such a position that I blushed all over my bald pate, and as a matter of course, I have to go and call on them as often as possible.

Say to your father that I often think of the many talks we have had about this country and other matters. I presume he and Gilbert play chess as much as ever and George---well, it keeps him busy taking care of his girl.

War news we know nothing about. Well, I must retire, and will finish tomorrow.

Thursday Morning

This is a lovely morning. I have had my breakfast and will rest all day so I will be in good shape for my journey tonight, and we may find a bear, moose, caribou or mountain sheep, before we get back at least. I hope so. One of the boys, Livengood, from Milan, killed a bear at Dawson and sold the meat for $1 per pound, and it dressed at 110 pounds. The skin he has tanned. I would like to run across a nice black bear or two just for the skins, but would rather kill a moose or caribou, for we are all anxious to get a taste of fresh meat. I had some moose meat a few days ago and it was simply fine.

Some of the rivers and creeks have plenty of fine fish, but the Yukon is so muddy all the time that there is no fish caught with hook and line, but a few are caught with nets, and this is an off year, and but few salmon are being caught, and those are caught by the Indians, and they ask $1 per pound. Prices for everything are coming down, but are yet high enough. I saw an ordinary lead pencil that cost $1 last winter, and the same pencil could be bought for 5¢ anywhere in the states. Eggs $18 a doz.; apples 50¢ a piece; tobacco, $8 a pound; meals, $3 and one ox sold for $14. These are last winter's prices, but now since the steamers have come up the river and so many men have sold out their outfits and gone home, everything is getting much cheaper.

I will be glad when we get our house done; it will seem more like living, and when it gets a little cooler so the mosquitoes are not so bad, I am going out to see if I can get some game.

You would smile to see some of the woman coming in over the trail, they dress just like men.

Now, Ed, write me a good long letter, and tell me all the news and how everybody is getting along. I would like to write to all of them, but I have not got the time, and then there is no certainty it would ever reach them. I know that you have plenty of time and are posted in to all that is going on. Remember me to all and especially the girls. I will longingly look for a good long letter at once. With kind regards and best of wishes for yourself and the rest of the people, I will remain.

Your Friend,

Dell J. Deyo

FROM GEORGE J. MILLER:

Eagle City, Alaska   July 25, 1898

Mr. W.L.Slate,

Sandusky

I received your letter some time ago, but on the same day that we left Dawson and we are now located here, with 12 front lots on the Yukon River and also with mines at Buckeye Creek and Lake Erie Springs, four miles up. We also have two good mines on the American river, which we suppose will pan out big as those adjoining us on both sides are giving out good sized nuggets.

We have been sawing lumber for sluice boxes for Buckeye creek, which will pan out all right, as the stream comes from the same hills as American creek. I have been out prospecting with a party if six besides myself. Huntington and Cowan came along but only stayed three days and then took two days rations for camp leaving me the balance to pack over the hills. We prospected several creeks and some of them had never been seen by a white man before, as the wood did not show a sign of the white man's axe or of fire. The boys named one of the creeks after me, so there will be a Miller Creek in Alaska and a tributary to Ryan Creek.

We went to the north fork of Forty Mile River a distance of about 25 miles from Eagle City, but we should have gone to Tannana and Copper River, if our grub hadn't given out. As it was, we were out 16 days and there wasn't a day that it didn't get wet down by rain. Of course, I didn't have a tarpaulin with me. The worst drenching was on the Bald mountains, where you couldn't get protection because there are no trees big enough to cover mosquitoes. We have sleeping bags into which we crawl after wrapping the blankets around us. Then we pull the flaps down over our faces and call ourselves housed for the night. Howard Huntington, Cowan and myself went up Last Chance creek some time ago and the mosquitoes were so bad that I crawled into the bag head foremost and then packed it close around my body and felt secure for a while. I had just told Howard that I had found a way to fool the mosquitoes when suddenly one of them gave me a peck that stirred me up to a fighting humor and made me get out of that bag quicker than I had gotten in. Then I got mad, pitched our tent and built a smudge that drove them all out. We slept until 11 o'clock next morning.

We are all in good health and are whipsawing lumber and slabbing logs for our cabin, which will be 50 by 20 feet and a story and a half high. Then we will have an additional 50 by 14 for our woodshed and cache, while making in all a house 50 by 34 feet.

We are waiting for a boom and when that comes we sell the balance of our lots, 11 in all, for a good round sum.

I will probably take a trip to Tannana, 150 miles, but I hope to have better luck the next time. Will Thompson, one of our crowd who went with me the last trip, was chief templer at Snohomish, Wash. He is up here with his brother and sister who is a schoolma'am. She has a lady friend, also a schoolma'am with her. They are nice people and have operated a bakery, picking up a good trade. You ought to see the Indians investing in pies from time to time. I believe they eat all they can of that luxury. Pies cost 60¢ each, bread 80¢ a loaf and doughnuts 5¢ each. Regards to all at the I.O.G.T. [46]

GEO. J. MILLER

---

[46] Good "Hot" Cabin in Cold Klondike, *The Sandusky Register,* 14 October 1898

From the Norwalk Daily Reflector:

Relatives and friends of members of the Sandusky party of twenty men who are in the Klondike country are greatly wrought up over reports received in letters that came yesterday and today.

There are complaints and serious ones at that, concerning the conduct of Captain Snevely, the leader, who was placed in charge of the expedition, sent out from Sandusky by the Alaska Co-operative Mining company on February 7. The men claim to be suffering for want of proper clothing and shoes, and the rigorous winter, with the thermometer going to 40 degrees below zero is rapidly setting in.

Jay and Ross Livengood, cousins, both of Milan, who are with the party, write that Capt. Snevely, who is in charge of all the funds and property, has been accused of grave things, and that like a man demented, he turned upon some of the boys, threatening to shoot them.

Letters have also been received in Sandusky from Messers Smith, Thiem, Meinzer and others, in which, complaints more or less bitter are made. Some of them are, perhaps, exaggerated, but all agree that there is something radically wrong with Snevely's management and that the party has been in financial straits and short of clothing.

The officers and members of the company at home are all anxious that their men in Alaska should have the best possible treatment, and a meeting will be held in the near future to discuss the situation. If the letters of credit have reached Capt. Snevely, he should have about $3,000 in his possession. It has been suggested, however that another letter of credit, for a good round sum, be sent to some member of the party other than Capt. Snevely, so that in case of any mismanagement on his part the hardy gold seekers need not suffer on account of it. At present all the claims, money and property of the company are in the name of Capt. Snevely, as agent, and he has full authority and control of them.

Since the above was put in type it has been learned that another letter, written by Wm. Thiem, has been received. It was dated August 7, and among other things states that the party was saved from dissolution only by the arrival of the delayed letter of credit from Circle City. Capt. Snevely is strongly censured. [47]

The following letter has just been received by Marshal Burton from Frank Adelman, who went to the Klondike last spring with the Sandusky party:

Dawson City,   Aug 3, 1898

Friend Marshal and Boys:

I will write you a letter from here, letting you know how I am getting along. Well, I never felt better and think I will stand it all right this winter, if I have lots of Boston strawberries and bacon to eat. We have not found that gold that we came up here for, but still

---

[47] The Klondikers, *The Norwalk Daily Reflector,* 5 October 1898

live in hopes. We have some claims in Eagle City, but I don't know if there is any gold in them. We will prospect them this winter.

Well, I wish I was home to go to war with the boys; they don't do a thing to them when they get after them. I got the Post Intelligence from Seattle of the 19th of August, with all the late war news. The papers come from Seattle in nine days, but they charge $1 for them; but we must have them to find out the war news.

There have been no strikes made here this summer yet, and lots of the men are selling out and going home again. Well, we will stay by it until next year, and then if we don't find anything we will do likewise.

Yours as Ever,

Frank A. Adleman

Seeing by paper clippings that you are going to get up a company of "Hobos" in Norwalk, I would like to join your company, for I will be a good "hobo" when I get back. [48]

Frank

Eagle City   Aug. 30

We landed here all right with the exception of the little difficulty I mentioned, but we have all compromised and everything is all right so far, it is Captain Snevely and Koegle now to go together and see to everything.

---

[48] From the Far North, *Norwalk Daily Reflector,* 5 October 1898

We got the box that was sent from Sandusky and were more than glad to get it, too, you can bet, for that box was filled with the best of novels and a book of Longfellow's poems, so you see we will have lots of reading this winter. Most of the boys got a letter and I got mine and all you sent me.

In camp on the Yukon.   Aug.30

Charlie Smith, George Gleckner and myself are on one of our claims sluicing. Things are going on as if nothing had happened. Captain and Koegle have gone to Circle City to get what is needed and the work goes on just the same. The boys are all feeling good. Confidence is restored.

Yesterday we were shoveling gravel all day and it has rained all day. Today we are in our shacks like a lot of Siwash Indians. We have a large fly that belongs to one of the tents stretched on a pole to serve as a tent. It is like a house with both ends knocked out and open from the ground for about two feet---oh, it is a warm place with plenty of light! We are sleeping on the ground and cooking outside. George is our cook and today he had it nice. It has rained hard all day and is quite cool, for winter is near at hand.

Charlie and Gleckner are rolled up in their blankets, fast asleep, but I could not sleep, so I am writing. In the box I got a letter from J.E. Bragg. Tell him when I have seen a little more of the country I will write him a good long letter. The mosquitoes are gone but the gnats give us a great plenty. They crawl all over us and when one bites you it raises a lump like a bee sting and forms a natural blister. I will be glad when they are gone. They are not bigger than the little end of nothing.

We will stay here until Saturday night and then go back to camp and Monday morning we will go out on Cuban ravine to prospect more claims out there. So this letter won't be mailed until Sunday. When the Captain gets back I will tell you all the news, so I will quit for this time, hoping to hear from you all soon, I am, as ever, your absent son.

JAY LIVENGOOD

The following good letters from William Theim and George J. Miller were sent from the Klondike, bringing all the news of the Sandusky party.

Eagle City, Alaska   Sept. 1.1898

Dear Mother and all:

I received your welcome letters and the Bible. The box arrived Aug. 25 I was very glad to hear from you all for every one of our crowd look for letters on every boat. Thanks for the Bible: it will be a good friend this winter. The summer here was warm and very pleasant, that is if the mosquitoes wouldn't bother us so. Now the days are getting short---daylight at 5 and night at 8.

Our cabin is nearly completed and is by far better than any cabin I have seen in this country. The roof, floor and ceiling will be of whip sawed lumber, the logs of the house are ripped in halves, and in this way the whole interior is a flat surface.

Eagle City is a pretty place located on the south bank of the Yukon and surrounded by sloping mountains. It has all prospects of being a good town, all creeks of importance empty into the Yukon near this point, and miners interested on creeks will certainly trade at the nearest post, Eagle City. Several transportation companies are building stores here which gives employment to quite a few men.

Mr. Barber, President McKinley's nephew, is in the country making a government survey. Their party is stopping near us and they visit our camp evenings and then we have concerts every night. Mr. Barber is a fine mandolin player and Howard Huntington accompanies him on the guitar.

We had a dance a week ago and there were only four women to about 200 men. I fared pretty well by getting four dances out of 15. We had a violin, mandolin, guitar, and mouth harp for dancing music, and the dance went on as smooth as any at home in the halls.

I have changed somewhat since I left home. I seem twice as old but look younger. I have gained weight and my hair is six inches long and as curly as it was when I was a little boy. I am well and have been all the time. There is no sickness at Eagle City, but Dawson is troubled with some kind of fever.

The work is hard but none of us have seen anything that we couldn't do. Part of the boys are out prospecting claims we have staked. We have not heard from them yet, but we know some are good as the claims above and below are paying well.

This country is healthy; the climate is dry, except in the rainy season, which is now on. When it freezes up in the fall it stays frozen until spring. Winter is the best season in this country, so the old miners say. The real cold weather such as 70 degrees below zero only lasts for a few days and the general average is from 25 to 35 below, and they consider zero thawing.

There are a couple of fishermen camped on the Yukon opposite us and they are catching a great many fish which are from two to four feet in length. They furnish us with 80 pounds a week at 5 cents a pound. That is as cheap as can be bought in the state. Game is also very plentiful, but there isn't much shot now for the warm weather would spoil it before it could be brought into camp.

I suppose everything is lively at home with a house full as you have now, and everyone enjoying themselves. I thought of the family picture, and I wished that I could have been home to have had it taken since all were home, but hope we can have it taken when I return. Does mother still like to cook? If she were to cook for us 20 men with our big appetites she would get tired of it in one day. All the mountains were full of berries and we had some very fine berry pie.

Tell little Clarence and Rolland I haven't found that big nugget yet, but they can gaze at the gold I sent in the letter until I find theirs.

I will close hoping you are all well and all will write soon. Give my best regards to all.

With Love,

WM THIEM

The news from the Sandusky-Klondike party is the following letters from Jay Livengood to his mother Mrs. Rose Livengood, Sand Hill. The latest date is Sept. 7, and all the letters were brought down by Mr. Barber, a nephew of President McKinley, and mailed at Seattle, Oct. 6. Mrs. Livengood kindly furnished these extracts to The Register for publication:[49]

Cuban Ravine, near Eagle City, Alaska,   Sept. 4

I thought I would write a few lines and tell you what we are doing now. Yesterday I was down to Eagle and mailed you a letter which I wrote you a week ago. The mail goes out only once in about three weeks and soon it won't get out that often, for the Yukon river will be frozen, so the boats will quit running and then the mail will have to be carried with dogs on sleighs. The mail that goes out every time the boat leaves now amounts to tons. The last mail that left Dawson was 27 sacks, so you see it will be quite a job to carry it up the river.

Today I am eight miles from headquarters, on a little creek called Cuban Ravine. It empties into the Yukon River. We loaded our baggage into the Arkansas yesterday afternoon and poled up the river, landed at 6 p.m., pitched our tent and commenced housekeeping again with Gleckner for cook. It was quite late before we got our tent up and supper ready and then we enjoyed a good night's rest for we were tired. This morning George was on deck first, got breakfast all ready and called Charlie Smith and myself. After eating a good meal Charlie and I went up the stream to see where would be the best place to prospect. We went about 15 miles and then turned back, tired and hungry, landing at camp at 5 o'clock. George had a good warm meal all ready for us and maybe

---

[49] They're Digging for Gold, *Sandusky Register,* 13 October 1898

we didn't fill ourselves up in a hurry. This is our bill of fare: A good big kettle of beans seasoned with bacon, coffee, good and strong, without sugar, and good light bread without butter. It was a meal good enough for a king.

When I mail this to you I will send some gold dust so you can see what we are after. I dare not send any big ones for fear you would not get them, but when I come home I will bring you one of the nicest pins you ever saw. It is a pick and shovel and gold pan and a little pair of scales with a little nugget on the scales. It is made at Dawson from pure gold. Will quit for today for it is getting quite dark and I have sat on my foot till it has gone to sleep.

September 5

Today is Labor Day and we did not work. I have been doing some washing for myself. It has been quite a nice day. The wind has been blowing hard. Glock and Charlie slept nearly all the forenoon. Charlie has taken a pan, shovel and pick and gone upstream to see if he could find any colors. Tomorrow we will commence to prospect this stream. We will keep sinking holes for a few days and see if there is anything in them worth washing. We have 20 claims on it of ten acres each and it is a good-looking stream. We will stay up here until Cap and Charlie get back from Circle City, and then I suppose we will go up to Buckeye creek and see what is on that. We have a number of claims there.

Ross and Frank Adelman are in the kitchen cooking for the boys at Eagle City, Perry and Pat are prospecting up at French Gulch. They have some good claims up there. Tomorrow night I will tell you what we find in our days search for gold.

Sept.7

Yesterday we sunk a hole on No. 2, 12 feet deep. We found good indications, so we had to stop to build a windlass to get the dirt out of the hole and Charlie and I had to go to Eagle city to get some ropes. It was only an eight mile walk and we got there a little while after dark, ate our supper and then went to a miners meeting. It was to decide if the people would allow newcomers to jump another man's lot and put up a cabin and claim it. The meeting was postponed till Friday evening at 7, when it will be decided.

Senator Allen of Illinois came near meeting death by the roof of his cabin falling in. Beaver and Anderson are his partners. They have a log cabin near us at Eagle City. They had just finished putting the dirt on the roof and Allen and Anderson were in the building when the roof fell in. Neither of them were hurt very badly, but they were scared good.

You can tell the boys they are not in it catching fish with the Indians. If they could see the Indians in a little birch bark canoe with a little dip net catching salmon as they float down the river, they would wonder. The Indians can tell when one is coming, and they will drop in a little net made of moose hide and flop them in their canoe.

They offered me a canoe and net to go out fishing, but they can't get me in that kind of a boat. One Indian wanted Charlie and myself to go moose hunting this morning. He saw three near our camp. One today was seen on a little island in front of our camp. We were not in, so we did not get a chance to shoot at it. Sunday morning we will try and see if we can find one. A neighbor just came in and I want to know what he knows about the streams that he is prospecting near us.

Sept. 11

Still in camp at Cuban ravine. We went down in claim No. 7, 19 feet and the water came in and we had to stop. We will go up to No. 1, and prospect that claim.

Last night when we got in who was there but Jimmy Houel standing in front of our camp. He had come down from Dawson. He saw our boat and stopped all night with us. We are going down to Eagle and will come back tonight. Jimmy will come back with us and stay for a day or two with us and go upstream and perhaps he will stake a claim or two. We are as happy as bluebirds up in the woods and hills. I think we will stay up here all winter. Well, I will quit for this time for I cannot think of much to write about.

Eagle City, Alaska.   Sept. 11, '98

A little insignificant gnat forced me to lay off from work yesterday for the first time. It stung me on the eyelid causing it to swell shut and affected both my eyes so that I could hardly see. I bathed it with boric acid and the swelling has now disappeared. I will be at work again tomorrow as we are very anxious to get our house done before the cold weather sets in. Another week, I think, will see us comfortably housed for the winter and we shall then commence hunting nuggets from our claims.

We heard yesterday of some rich finds on the American river near where some of our claims are located. When the news reached us, Howard Huntington and Billy Cowan dropped their whipsaw, threw some food into their pack and started, saying they would probably be back by night. They have not yet returned, so I am unable to say at this time what they have done.

Capt. Snevely and Charles Koegle have not returned from Circle City, but we expect them now at any time. A steamboat just now made a landing near my tent to unload 43 tons of merchandise for a new store that is going up just above us. There will be three stores open here this winter and plenty of provisions. One of the men just came in with his pockets full of nice large onions and handed me one, the first I have seen since I left Seattle. I asked him where he got them and he said, "I didn't steal them, I just reached in the box and took them." Another man has just gone to see how deep he can reach in the box. Onions are quite cheap, selling for about 50 cents a pound.

There is quite an amount of fruit to be had at Dawson City if one only has the price. Watermelons are from $5 to $10 each, bananas $1 each, apples 25 cents, oranges $3 per dozen and other fruits in the same proportion. We bought 50 pounds of sugar the other day at 50 cents a pound. Fish is the cheapest article of food in this section at present, having dropped from $1 per pound to 5 cents. We have a contract with a man to furnish us with 100 pounds a week, 50 pounds on Monday and Friday, as long as he can catch them. The run of salmon is now nearly over.

Howard Huntington is the only one of the party who has received a letter addressed to Eagle City. His letter from home was dated Aug. 8 and was 24 days on the road. Our mail is delayed somewhere on the road and will probably get here in the next mail which is due about the 15th or 18th.

The weather here now is like the latter part of October in Ohio. The leaves have turned yellow except the spruce which are always green and are falling fast, and the nights are frosty and there is more or less drizzling rain during the day. The boats on their down trip are looking for winter quarters, there is quite a number of them bound up, and many will not be able to reach Dawson this season.

About 75 steamboats passed this place this summer. Some that were on the river last season made three trips to Dawson from St. Michaels this season. Those that came in this season have been delayed so long at St. Michaels getting in shape after their ocean voyage of 2,300 miles that they won't all get up the river this fall.

The fare from Dawson to Seattle or San Francisco is $200 first class and not much, if any, difference from here. We are 117 miles north of Dawson; about eight hours run for one of these river boats downstream. The current was nearly six miles an hour which is all right coming down but a different proposition going up. It took some of the boats 20 days to get up, though the steamer Hannah made it in a little less than 13 days. Twenty days is considered a good run for the 1,600 miles from tidewater to Dawson.

Howard Huntington received some film for his camera in the box from home and has filled up the roll. He sends it out with this mail so you can soon see some views from Eagle City. They are sent to Osberg's.

After nearly a month of silence on the part of the Sandusky party in the Klondike, word again came to the Register announcing the continued health of all, received by Charles Livengood from his brother Jay:

Eagle City   September 24.

Dear Brother Charlie:

   I will now attempt to answer your kind and welcome letter,
which, since its receipt, I have read so many times that its contents
are thoroughly committed to memory. I should have written before,
but remember that old adage---Better late than never--- and
pardon me this time.

Our summers experience has been great indeed, and the sights
we have seen are beyond my ability to tell, so this letter must be
confined to present conditions. The weather though has been
bearable, at times quite hot and on one occasion the temperature
reached 94 in the shade, weather that in old Erie County would have
been considered excellent hay weather. Still, one had but to lift the
moss and ice could be found at any place. On July 4, in a little gulch
I walked on ice between 12 and 14 inches in thickness. I expect
before the winter is over to walk on ice much thicker, and fear the
time is not far distant either. At this time last year the Yukon was
frozen up, but boats are still running. Lots of them will never reach
Dawson this season, and many will not see St. Michaels.

   I am still living in a tent on Cuban ravine. Charlie Smith and I
have for the past week been fishing, and with excellent success. I
finished pulling in a large barrel today, a catch that would beat
Grover's at Middle Bass. We caught 24 big salmon using for the
purpose a small dip net on a long pole. The Yukon is an awfully dirty
stream and the fish swim near the shore leaving a ripple in the water
by which you know of their approach. We drop the net when the fish
comes opposite and haul him in. Charlie and I caught on to this
wrinkle by watching the Indians, who are successful fishers, and we

rigged up a similar contrivance. Already we have caught in the neighborhood of 300 pounds. We are drying a great deal of the catch for winter use. We want some for dog feed also. We have a dog and seven puppies, dandies a cross between the Husky and the timber wolf, called Malamutes.

The boys are still working on their cabin and it is nearly finished. Charlie and I will put one up as soon as our fishing is over, we can then prospect in the ravine. Howard and Cowan are over on Welsh creek sinking now.

We had a lady caller today for dinner, an old lady with whom we became acquainted with at Dawson. She wanted to cross the river to look at a small stream on the opposite and stake a claim, Charlie took her across and later accompanied her to Eagle and has not yet returned. The old lady gave us a very cordial invitation to dine with her Sunday, suggesting that she would have krout, and I think we will go for I hate to let a good meal go begging---that you know. I will give you my bill of fare for supper, as ate alone tonight: Fried fish, fish liver and hearts with onions, potatoes, beans, stewed peaches, biscuits and coffee that is plenty good for an Alaska Meal.

We have not yet struck gold but expect to this winter. Because of the water, not much in that line can be done in the summer. The winter is the only time to do work of that sort in this country. It is no little chore to get your grub over the hills to where you want to prospect and as soon as the snow gets deep enough we will commence to do some sledding, and in the spring I hope to tell you luck or success has crowned our efforts.

Charlie and I go down to Eagle on Sunday next taking with us a boatload of fish. I wish you at home might have some. The boys at

Eagle want them at every meal and we take them a lot on every visit. Sunday the boys will be looking for us and I think we will have Howard take a snapshot of us and our catch so you at home can see that our stories are not magnified. The different fish caught here are salmon, grayling, herring, white fish and suckers; the latter are as boney as those at home. These are all the kinds I have run across. My candle is nearly out so I will quit and write again tomorrow.

September 25

The night was one continual storm, but the sun is out again this morning, the weather is, excepting for a steady hard wind, the latter heavy enough to put fishing out of the question, and up to this time---noon, our combined catch has been ten only. We will load the Arkansas this afternoon putting in 75 partially dried, a barrel of 'em salted and a few well dried fish.

How are all the boys at the Corners, I presume the same old gang gather at Parker's and fill the room with smoke as of yore. Don said he would write and tell of those evening gatherings, but some seductive influence must have led him astray for I have yet to hear from him.

Give my love to mother and tell her not to worry as I am all right and will neither freeze nor starve. Remember me to all friends.

Your Brother,

JAY

Sylvester Widman's letter From Eagle City:

Eagle City, Alaska,   Oct.10, 1898

To Wolf Bros. Fremont Ohio

Dear Friends:

I will take the opportunity and write you a few lines as I had promised. There was no mail going out from here for two months, and now I do not know how soon it will go, but next year we will have better mail service; we will have mail here every two weeks. I guess you have been wondering where I was and what I am doing, or how I am getting along. I often think of you and the pleasant chats we have had. As far as prosperity is concerned I would say that it is by far better than in the states. A common day laborer gets $10 per day, and if anyone refuses to pay, the miners will have a meeting and make him pay $10 as agreed. The Northwestern Transportation and Trading Company was going to pay their men $7.50 per day, but the miners held a meeting and made them pay the full amount. In regard to Eagle City I would say that it has a population of about 1,000 people, only 23 of them woman, about 300 houses, eight stores and three saloons. The first house built in Eagle City was in May last. We have the finest and largest dwelling in Eagle; it is 20x50, with a wing 12x50, ceilings ten feet high, ornamented. Some build solid and substantial with a piazza and the United States flag waving from the roof, with an extra bunting marked "Sandusky Headquarters."

There is only one creek here that has been opened, called American Creek, which proves very good. Every claim that has been opened on it has paid well. We have two claims on American creek which are all right. There are many other creeks that are, or seem to be, all right; we do not know just how good, as they have not been explored, but we are certain that there is gold there. We have the honor of naming three creeks--- Buckeye, Castalia and Cuban Ravine. We have a number of claims on every one of those creeks named, and some on others. We have all together about 60 claims, but have not done much mining yet, mostly prospecting, looking up claims, building a house and other work, so we can work our claims more successfully this winter, and I think we will take out some money next spring.

I have been running a sawmill for a lumber company, but we are now through for this fall. I will go moose hunting just as soon as we get some snow. Game of all kinds is plenty here even muskrats. Fishing is very good in the Yukon River; we caught a good many salmon; we hang them up to dry. They weigh from 10 to 20 pounds. A large salmon which is only found in the mouth of the Yukon in the month of July weighs from 20 to 60 pounds, but we are not fixed for them.

In speaking of the weather, I would say that it is very fine; so far we have not had any cold weather. We had a few hard frosts, but it is not much colder than it is in Ohio at this time of year. I am told that it will freeze up here about November 1st. I am also told that last winter they could work all but about three or four days, so you see that it is not so cold as people and newspapers claim it is, in the states.

Now, how about politics; is it quite hot this fall? Are they making many speeches? I wish I was with them again to help them make speeches. Please tell me all about it.

And now about the war; I understand it is all over, and how many of the Fremont boys had the grit to enlist? Please send me a list of them.

In regard to people coming out here, I would not encourage anybody to come, although the country is all right and is much better than the states. If anyone comes here he must expect to stay from three to five years; if anyone stays that long he will be sure of making a fortune of some size, especially if he minds his business and works. Hundreds and thousands are coming out here, and when they do not see any fortune inside of a week or two they take the first boat and go back to the states again, and claim the country is no good.

In regard to the Dawson gold fields, I would say that they are rather small. There are a few good claims but all are taken; besides an American does not stand any show. We stayed in Dawson ten days and left six of our men there for three months, but they did not get anything of value. In the summertime it is just as warm as in Ohio, and the mosquitoes are quite bad for about two months. We wore mosquito netting over our faces and gloves with long cuffs, to keep them off. In the summer there is no darkness for three months; the days now are just as long as in Ohio, but in about six weeks they will be only about four or five hours long.

Last night we had some visitors, among then five ladies, one of them a very fine violinist. I assisted playing while the rest were having a jolly time dancing. We had a fine time. There is a fellow here from Fremont, whose name is Frank Wegstein. He is a cousin to Will Falter and sends his regards to Will and his folks and all his other friends in Fremont.

I expect to be in Fremont in one year from now, then I can tell you more in one hour as much about Alaska as I can write in one week. One of our boys came home from duck hunting and brought 70 ducks. I asked an Indian how many times he would shoot at a moose and he said, "One shot one moose." When they go after a moose they make a sure thing of it. They are a large animal weighing from 600 to1000 pounds. Their skin will make a valve 10x10 and their horns weigh up to 100 pounds.

There are about 100 steamboats on the Yukon River; they run between St. Michael's and Dawson but can make only one or two trips in a season.

If anyone from Fremont wants to come out here I would say they would do well by taking horses along; but burros are far better, as they can stand the hardships of the rough journeys better and are better adapted to carry pack over the trails. The Skagway trail is for winter and the Dyea trail for summer.

I must now bring my writing to a close for this time, in wishing you all a merry Christmas and a happy New Year. My best wishes to you and all the boys.[50]

Yours Very Truly,

Sylvester Widman

---

[50] Sylvester Widman, *Norwalk Daily Reflector,* 19 January 1899

The following letter from the Cleveland World, written by W.F. Reid of Dawson City, while not referring to the Sandusky party in the Klondike, will be of particular interest to those who have friends in the north since the existing conditions which affect the writer must certainly affect all who reside in the locality:

Dawson City, Alaska   October 20, 1898

A month ahead is a long time ahead on Thanksgiving dinner, but by the time you receive this Thanksgiving dinner will have been eaten. We are not going to go hungry, but we don't expect the usual turkey, for its doubtful if one could be secured up here for love or money.

Some things are getting scarce already and navigation is hardly closed. Durham tobacco is selling for $6 a pound, mortise locks at $8 apiece, window glass, according to size, 8x10, $2, and from that up.

Bacon sells for 50 cents a pound; sugar 30 cents, etc; evaporated potatoes, 75 cents; onions, 75 cents; canned goods, 50 cents to $2 a can; flour, $8 per sack; oil, $1.50 per gallon; candles, $6 per box; brooms, $3 each; ordinary lamps, $6 and $8; shoes, such as would sell for $1.50, they soak us $6, and $4 when you want them half-soled; a good wash board can be bought for $2.50; washtub, $5; wringers, $13.

Clothing has advanced 50 percent since the cold weather set in. During the summer it could be bought at your own price. The town is feeling the effect of the miners going to their winter's work.

Hundreds of them are to be seen packing their goods to the mines, using pack mules, horses and dogs.

Good dogs are from one to two hundred dollars. Feed is too expensive to permit the keeping of horses.

Prices on provisions continue high. A month ago I was commissioned by a Mr. Brewitt to buy a lot of butter and condensed milk. I paid $1,400 for the lot, which today would sell for $14,000. That is the way they do business in Dawson.

The theaters are running full blast. They have their brass bands, posters, etc., the same as at home, and the houses are crowded every night.

The combination theater receipts amount to over $1,000 every night and the bar contributes another thousand.

The banks will loan you all the money you want with the best mining property as security, at 10 percent a month. From a business standpoint the town cannot be beat.

I was up at Eldorado creek yesterday to see George Mallory of Bucyrus, O. He is representing his brother's interest on claim No. 12. They were very busy getting ready for the winter's work. No. 13 is one of the richest claims on Eldorado, 320 feet of the 500, having been worked out and averaging $2,000 to the foot, and they expect to work the remainder 180 feet this winter.

The Bucyrus boys have taken lays on Chicken creek and expect to clean up $5,000 apiece. The miners here don't usually own their own lays. The owner of the claim gives you 50 feet of ground to work, and you get a certain percent of the gross cleanup.

Mining is no snap here and it is hard work to get the gold from the frozen creek beds.

Usually, the place selected to begin operations is the extreme limit of the claim, so that your dumps will not be interfering with your future work and that all the ground will be thoroughly worked and none of it is missed.

Two holes are sunk one at either corner of the claim. It requires about 10 days to put a hole down 20 feet.

To sink a hole, fires are built on a space the size of the hole. One fire will thaw from six inches to one and a half feet, according to the nature of the ground. When the two holes are down to bed rock and the pay streak located, the two forces work toward the center of the claim, thus cleaning out about 10 feet wide.

All the pay dirt is removed and put on dumps. This work continues until the spring thaw stops work underground; then commences the work of sluicing your dump. If the supply of water is not at hand, flumes must be built to bring the water near your dump and into the sluice box.

Sluice boxes are a series of boxes with strips nailed crosswise on the bottom. The first is longer and wider than the others and into this one the dirt is shoveled. A good head of water is kept running over the dirt and all the gold settles to the bottom and is caught by the strips.

A clean-up is made every 24 hours, except when a mine is exceedingly rich and there is danger of the gold running over the strips, then a clean-up is made twice a day.

The gold in the sluice boxes contains black sand and must be put into a gold pan and washed by hand, a simple process if you only have the gold. Where gold is very fine, quicksilver is used, but gold here is all coarse and can be thoroughly cleaned by hand.

After the gold is washed, it is dried by heating on the stove, and then put into a moose hide sack and ready to be spent, and it doesn't take the average miner long to spend it.

It is getting cold very fast, and the ice is forming on the river, but the weather is clear and fine. The lowest the thermometer has registered is ten above zero, on October 3, but everything will be pretty well frozen up by the end of the month.[51]

The following letter was received by Mrs. Rose Livengood of Milan from her son Jay, of Cuban Ravine, Klondike.

Cuban Ravine,   Oct. 16, 1898

Dear Mother:

It is time I wrote you a few lines and though there is but little to write about I will do the best I can. The boys at Eagle City have finished their cabin and moved into it. It is very comfortable and convenient; has a row of bunks in each side of the main room and a long table between the bunks; two long benches, one either side of the table. At one end of the room is the cooking department; at the other is the big drum stove, some small tables at which to read and

---

[51] Klondike Prices, *Sandusky Daily Register,* 28 November 1898

write and play cards on. The cook has everything handy and a nice cast iron cook stove with everything convenient around him; cupboard, table and the cache to his right--- all he has tot do is open the door and he is the only one that can do so as he alone has the key.

Frank is the cook now, but he won't be there long, as he is coming to spend the winter with us. We have finished our new home and it is a dandy I tell you--- 13X16 on the inside---made of spruce logs well mossed between the joints. The floor is of the same material, well laid, then adzed down smooth. Our roof boards are of the same with poles and shingled, and six inches of mother earth. We have a porch extending six feet out over our front door, the door is cased with good, whipsawed lumber worth one dollar per square foot--- none of your cheap stuff as you will observe. We have a door to match. Our hinges are made from a piece of old Berry's tug. We will soon be eating with our feet under a table and have a nice bench to sit on. We will sleep in a nice bunk made of nice smooth spruce poles. Our springs won't break and our feather tucks will be in our dreams, but one thing we will have is a good lot of grass in the bottom of our bunks that will beat the frozen earth all to pieces. It will be the first time in six months that I have slept off the ground, excepting when we slept in the snow. I shall make a good strong chair to rest on when I come in from work, and a nice little table to write on, one that I can fasten to the side of the cabin. I am now writing on a piece of sole leather that came from Capt. Parson's store in Sandusky.   It is so cool in our tent tonight that the ink freezes on my pen so I can hardly write, so I think I will quit and finish in the morning.

It is much warmer this morning. George Gleckner has been writing all the forenoon while I have been doing some patching and it is near dinner time. The drift ice has been coming down the river in great sheets that means the river will soon freeze over now and the boats have already stopped running.

It is not safe for one to start across the river in a boat now as it would be smashed to pieces in an instant. Ross is on the Buckeye building a cabin with Pat McCrystal and Henry Zurcher, where they will live this winter while prospecting. Howard, Cowan, Thiem and Fettle are building a cabin on the Yukon for the party to live in while cutting wood this winter. The barber, Perry Hutchins, is working at his trade in Eagle City. A.B. Sanderson has just got back from a duck hunt down the river, he brought 70 of them back with him and when Charlie gets back to camp we will have duck for dinner. Widman, for the past week has been head sawyer in the sawmill at Eagle City. A week ago tonight the Eagle City folks gave the Buckeye boys quite a surprise, a goodly crowd soon gathered and it was not long before we could hear "Head couple lead to the right, change, swing half way." Good music was there, and this lasted till 1a.m. The Eagle City boys brought their bottles, but I will drop the curtain, the event will long be remembered by the Buckeye boys. Eagle City is growing fast the population is estimated between 2,500 to 3,000. Charlie's catch of fish and my own went to Eagle City last week, we had about 500 salmon, but we will do better next summer.

October 19

We are now living in our new cabin, moved in Monday. We have been sledding our goods up to the cabin and finished this morning. There is four inches of snow now and still snowing. Ross came over from Buckeye; he said it was very slippery crossing the mountains. He came to get the adz to smooth their floor as it is like ours---made of poles. We banked our cabin up today with dirt so you can see but four logs on a side. It is a warm affair I tell you. When we get a good fire going we have to open the door or we would melt. So I don't think you will have to worry about us, as we will be as warm here as we would be at home. I tell you it seems like living at home where you can put your feet under a table, although it is not a walnut or cherry with carved legs. Our table is two boards, 10 inches wide by eight feet long, not planed, with pole legs, and we have two good benches to match. Next week we will begin to tear up the dirt and sink as many shafts as we can along Cuban Ravine hoping to find some of that yellow metal we are working so hard to get. We find good color at the surface but can't tell what lays at bed rock until we dig down. If there is any we are bound to find it at bed rock and the other boys will do the same on the other streams. It seems to me we are bound to strike it, it has been found on every side of us, so I think we will come out on top. In the spring the water bothered us so or we would have known before this time how we stood. It has not frozen quite deep enough yet, but we will go to sinking holes and perhaps by that time it will be frozen so we can keep at work all the time. I hope so anyhow for lying around is rough on your pants and I don't like to mend them, that you know, don't you mother? Oh, yes, by the way, I think I forgot to tell you about our windows. We have two of them made of whisky bottles, seven in each window from the Buckeye jamboree. Part of them are brown, part white, so you see we have all colors, and when old Sol gets in his best licks I don't think we will have to drop the window curtains do you.

October 22

This is Friday and tomorrow some of the boys are going to Eagle City, and I thought I would try and finish this so they can mail it for me. It has been snowing for the last five days and is 14 inches on the level. The snow is almost as fine as flour, when it falls you hardly see it, it is more like a fog or fine mist and the ground has not frozen much yet. What is the reason you don't write oftener? I suppose you do, though the mails are so uncertain about going out that I don't know when you will get this, if ever, but I hope you will so you won't worry about me as I know you do. I am all right you can depend on it. The only things I want right now is some two cent stamps and a million dollars, and then I will be ready to come home. Well, mother and the rest of you, when you write tell me how everything is back home and around the corners. Tell Mr. Parker that I would like to spend one evening at the store to help fill the room with smoke like we did some months ago.

Hoping this will find you and the boys as well as it leaves me, I will close with best regards to all inquiring friends. I remain as ever,[52]

Your son,

Jay Livengood

---

[52] In Cold Alaska, *Norwalk Daily Reflector,* 13 January 1899

The Miner's Court

For some time there had been rumors upon the street of serious dissensions in the camp of the Sandusky men who went to the Klondike, which same dissensions had their counterpart in this city where the business of the company is done. Something was wrong but just what it was no one knew, as the directors of the mining company refused to talk upon the subject.

The last batch of letters from the frozen country contained some startling revelations. The letter printed in part below gives a lucid account of the misdeeds of Capt. Snevely, who oversaw the company. The story of his betrayal of his companions, the flashing of revolvers and the rough court is one that shows how sadly the confidence of the people who entrusted him with their money and their loved ones, was misplaced (Appendix B). The stern justice of the miner's court was not blocked by any legal formalities, and the Judas of the company met with his deserts.

For certain reasons not all of the letter is printed. Suffice to say that the parts omitted contain a direct charge of fraud upon a man who is on the inside of things here. Fraudulent entries and open embezzlement are charged and moreover, the letter says that the letters of this man at Sandusky taken from him at the miners' court sustain the charges. Certified copies of these letters came with the last mail and were the cause of the calling of a meeting of the Klondike directors at the Slone house last Friday night. A warm time was had at this meeting. It is rumored that several of the men lost their heads and became very badly excited. It is understood that certain law books were thrown and that a general mix-up followed, which it took the cooler headed men some time to quiet.

H.C. Huntington and John F. McCrystal, who have the unlimited confidence of the miners, were added to the directors. The board is now trying to settle things and keep quiet a series of frauds by men at the mention of whose names in such connections Sandusky people would stand back aghast. The letter is as follows:

Eagle City,   Nov. 18, 1899

Since writing you last under date Nov. 5th, we have had a rather lively time in our camp. You will remember some time ago I wrote you that there was more or less dissatisfaction in our party in regard to our manager, J.E. Snevely, but that he had agreed to our terms and everything would come out all right. We did not know our man although we had been keeping tab on him since leaving Skagway where our trouble commenced. Before we left Sandusky, the board of directors appointed C.W. Koegle and Sylvester Widman, in connection with Snevely as an advisory board, to act in conjunction with each other in all business of importance, but the fact is that at no time since we left home has Snevely consulted either of the above named gentlemen in the manner intended, but has gone ahead on his own way, squandering and spending ours and the company's money regardless of anything we might say. On the trail from Skagway to Bennett City the only work that he did was to carry three sacks of flour over Porcupine Hill. The rest of the time was spent telling people on the trail of his experience in Alaska, while the truth is that he never was in Alaska further than Juneau and Sitka, both places on the coast. As a mining engineer he is a complete failure, making himself the laughingstock of all the miners he comes in contact with. Lying and deception are his whole stock in trade.

Our first serious trouble with him was at Bennett City, when he refused to pay a man an honest debt he had contracted, amounting to $98. We advised him to settle, but in his bull headed way he refused, making it necessary to fight a lawsuit which cost him $11 more than the bill. Then a few days after he takes a junketing trip to Sitka, leaving us for 5 days to work as we saw fit, taking a trip that probably cost him $150, which he admitted to J.L. Shay that he did not have to make, as he had received a letter stating that the business he was going on had been attended to by mail, also saying it was none of the boys business where he went. Besides, he told the judge of other matters he wanted to go to Sitka for of which I need make no mention.

His next move was to get into trouble with the mounted police. When we landed our boat, we hoisted our flag and left it flying at the mast head. A short time after a policeman came to the boat and in a gentlemanly way informed the captain that we were flying our flag contrary to Canadian laws, that if we wanted to keep it up we should hoist the Canadian jack over it. He refused to do this in an insolent manner. The officer told him he was not there to argue the matter but if it was not taken down at once he would send over a squad of men to take it down, and also take him. He paid no attention to it but said the United States government would stand by him. We thought different and to save further trouble and expense, George Miller lowered the flag.

From that time the police were on him until we reached Dawson. He has made enemies all along the line and not one friend to our knowledge. At our meeting in August we told him in very plain language that he must come down off from his high horse or resign as manager; that we would no longer put up with the way he was acting. We knew he was crooked but had no proof of it at that time. He readily consented to all we asked of him, even to having Charles Koegle accompany him to Circle City to purchase our winters supplies, or part of them at least.

We mistrusted that if he should go alone we would not see him again, so we concluded that it was best to have Charlie go with him. For a short time after he returned we thought he intended to do better by us, but it was not long that we saw by his actions that something was wrong; that he was up to some scheme to do us. Well to make a long story short, he began to hint that he had to go to Dawson to get a rebate on duties paid at the summit and when all but three of the boys were away he told Charlie he was going. Charlie objected, telling him he did not think it was necessary, besides our money was nearly exhausted and that we might need what we had before spring. However, he started taking with him the two dogs and two weeks grub, In company with 11 other men and one woman—unlucky 13. The first day out they became snowbound nine miles up on the Yukon and as the cabin they stopped at was too small for the whole party, the captain went to one of our cabins about a mile further on, where Huntington and several more of the boys were chopping wood. Howard mistrusted that something was wrong, and he and Charlie Smith took a run in to make a few inquiries and found that as Cap had said he could not make a confidant of any of the men, he could confide in the prostitutes of the town. He told them he intended to go back to the states. They had told others and the boys heard of it. They went and saw the woman, one of whom was with the party going to Dawson. She said it was true that he had told her of his intentions. They were snow bound three or four days and during that time Howard had got 11 of the boys on hand the morning that the party moved on. They told Snevely that they wanted him to defer his trip and go back with them to Eagle City and explain matters. He refused to go, drew a large 44-caliber Colt's revolver and threatened to shoot them if they would not let him pass.

Judge Shay was spokesman of the party and stepped in front of him, when Judas E. said, "Stand back Judge, or I'll shoot you." The Judge replied, "Captain, don't you know that you are violating your contract by carrying that gun? You are the only man in the party that has one. On your own motion it was made a law not to carry concealed weapons in our party, but you have paraded around all summer with one strapped onto you. Now we are determined that you do not go to Dawson without first coming back to Eagle and making an explanation. You haven't bullets enough to kill all of us, so come along quietly and put up your gun."

He concluded this was the best thing to do and came down with them but before reaching Eagle he hastened his speed, leaving his sled and dogs with the boys. He rushed by our cabin and into the custom house and in a very tragic way exclaimed; "Mr. Cody, I throw myself and property into your keeping, as a United States officer, for protection against these robbers who have held me up and have interfered with the United States mails (he had three or four private letters that he was taking out) They have tried to assassinate me and I need your protection." Mr. Cody replied, "If you want my protection, you must hand over your gun."

The boys requested Mr. Cody to hold the papers and money turned over to him which belonged to the Alaska Co-operative mining company until such time as he would be requested to so do by the proper authorities. He said he would. We tried to have a settlement with him without making our troubles public but could do nothing with him. We posted notices for a miners and citizens meeting to be held Monday evening, Nov. 14 to decide whether or not we should have the property. The judge stated our case just as it was at the meeting. Judas pled his own case, as he could not get an attorney to act for him. The consequence was that on a vote being taken the Buckeye boys were given the decision by a unanimous vote, and all the company's property was turned over to C.W. Koegle, manager of the Alaska Co-operative Mining company, by the chairman and secretary. At the meeting we announced that we had offered J.E. Snevely $50 and 40 days grub to help him out of the country. Someone put this as a motion, and we gave him this amount.

Last Saturday the boys held a meeting to decide how much we ought to give him, provided he would accept. The proposal above was carried by a vote of 13 to 6. I want to go down on record as one who voted "no."

A man who would deliberately leave a party of men in a country like this with insufficient food, taking all the money, papers and records of the company, besides stealing money we had earned and which he held in trust I say I could see such a man freeze or starve before I would help him. This fall Mr. Widman earned $80 by running a sawmill eight days, and in accordance with our contract, he gave Snevely the check for the amount. This Snevely drew and afterwards lied about intending to keep it.

Here follows some statements, referred to in the introduction, which show that Snevely was in collusion with certain men in this city, members of the company, to defraud the other members of the company. The story of the stolen grip is told but with a different interpretation. The Klondikers believe that Snevely stole it himself as a blind to cover the criminal acts of himself and his associates.

We also find that he received $500 at Dawson which Mr. Huntington had informed Howard had been sent him. We asked him several times about this draft, and he always denied having any knowledge of it, while we have the word of a personal friend that he received the money from the bank in Dawson. We also have proof that he intercepted three letters that were given him at Dawson for Howard Huntington because he believed Mr. Huntington was writing something to Howard that he did not want us to know. The acts of this damnable scoundrel have ended in a terrible calamity, not only to us but to poor Judge Shay, who looked into the muzzle of his revolver. The worry and strain before and after the trial so worked on the judge that he lost his mind and is now a---------RAVEING MANIAC.

It takes two men all the time to take care of him. The doctor says there is not much hope for him and advises us to put up a padded cell in our cabin where he cannot get out or do himself any injury. Our hears all go out to him, as he was a nice, pleasant fellow, and we all intend to do all we can for him and try to make his condition as comfortable as possible. It is impossible to send him out of the country at this time of the year, as it is 750 miles from here to Dyea and the thermometer all the past week has been from 40 to 60 degrees below zero. Some men hardly dare to undertake a trip of this kind and will freeze themselves without knowing it, so what would become of a poor crazy man? We will have to keep him here and do the best we can, although we do not get much rest as he keeps up a continual chatter night and day. One minute he is the czar of Russia, the next McKinley, God or some other person—a most pitiable sight.

Miller and I intend to start off for our cabin tomorrow if the weather moderates a little. We do not want to start if it is below 40, as it is dangerous. We cannot feel the cold until frozen. It is a queer sensation when it is below 60. When you step out and inhale the air is like inhaling hot steam, a burning sensation which makes you catch your breath. It is no place for week lungs. Your breath freezes about one foot ahead of you with a crackling noise. When you throw out a pan of water it cracks like a firecracker when it comes in contact with the cold air and is frozen before it touches the ground. I commenced this letter Thursday but did not get a chance to finish it until tonight, (Sunday) on account of the confusion caused by the judge. Perry Hutchins, his bunk mate from the start, is watching with him tonight, and can do more to quiet him than anyone else. The mail leaves tomorrow, weather permitting. We have had no mail since Oct. 1. It is expected now at any time, and I hope I get news from home. I would rather get a letter from you than to find a ten-pound nugget. This trouble has delayed us some, but we will be straightened out soon with Charlie Koegle in command and the hearty co-operation of all the boys.

None of us have reached bed rock yet but some of the boys think they are near it as they have one hole down 15 feet.[53]

    Howard Huntington

---

[53] Betrays Comrades, *The Sandusky Star Journal,* 19 January 1899

SNEVELY DEPOSED

The letter comes with some remarks of a private nature and only of interest to the recipients.

.A letter written by Dell Deyo of the Sandusky-Klondike party, under date of November 25, had been received by John S. Speer. The letter gives an excellent story of the sensational events which led up to the deposing of Captain Snevely.

At the miner's trial Captain Snevely was ordered to leave the country, and was given 40 days rations and $50 in money. At the writing of this letter, he was currently on his way there.

In his letter, Mr. Deyo makes some rather sensational statements involving local people, which for good reasons cannot be made public. He begins his letter by saying that all of the party, with the exception of Judge Shay, are well. The thermometer ranges from 20 to 60 degrees below zero, and the days are all but five hours long. He then says:

Well, I have never written you or any of my friends but that we are progressing finely. So we are, with one exception. We have discovered that our manager, Mr. Snevely was a fraud and crook of the lowest order, consequently we have watched his every move and our success and the keeping of the party all together is due to a few of us who have managed to keep the balance in line until the proper time came, well knowing that come it would, sooner or later. It came and Snevely is now on his way out.

Snevely has never considered the advisory board, consisting of Koegle and Widman, but has always taken a csar-like position and considered us as mere hirelings and not a part of the company, and, in fact, the main part of the company.

About four weeks ago he informed us that he was going up to Dawson to collect some duty money due us, but we had every reason to believe he was going to Seattle and from there to Sandusky. He got everything ready and started with the only dogs we had, and we let him go. Through a woman in Eagle City, it was learned that this was his real intentions. We at once determined that he should return to Eagle City, and as good luck would have it, it stormed so hard next day that Snevely and his party could not travel, and our boys took advantage of the situation and immediately notified the boys at Cuban Ravine and Buckeye Creek. All were on hand early next morning, eleven in all. They quietly informed Snevely of their request, and he at once said he would return with them to Eagle and went ahead and got his sled ready, and before the boys were aware of it, he had it down the bank on the trail and heading for Dawson. The boys at once stepped in and told him they were in earnest; and that he had to return to Eagle with them, and that the best thing for him was to do so quietly and settle the matter without anyone outside our own party knowing anything about it.

Snevely at once drew a 44-colt revolver and ordered them to stand back and not interfere with his property. The boys at once informed Snevely that none of them were armed and that he did not have enough bullets to kill all of them, and he was sure to lose his own life. They finally shamed him out of it. He put up his revolver and all hands started for Eagle. All went well until within about two miles of our home here, when Snevely commenced to walk faster and faster, but Huntington kept ahead, and when Huntington came up the bank to our house Snevely immediately started on a run down to the end of the town and our lads after him.

Snevely went to the United States Customs officer and demanded protection. Our boys told the officer that they had no desire to hurt Snevely but requested him to hold all monies papers and property of every kind on Snevely's person as to such time as the matter could be finally settled. We sent out for the balance of our men, hoping to make some kind of settlement among ourselves, but if not, we would call a citizens meeting. We appointed a committee to call on Snevely and exhausted every effort to compromise, but he was bound to have a meeting and we knew what the result would be, for all of our boys have many friends here while Snevely has none and it is a fact, if the citizens had not stood in awe of us 19 men back of Snevely, they, the citizens, would have sent him down the river a long time ago. We, as a last resort, called a meeting, and there were about 300 men present. They heard both sides of the case as well as the contract, and Mr. Koegle's credentials making him our manager, if at any time Snevely was out of the way. According to the terms if the contract, Snevely has forfeited all rights in this company, and is forever and eternally out of it.

By a unanimous vote, they decided to have all money, papers and property of every kind belonging in any way to the company or pertaining in any way to the business of the company, to be turned over to Mr. Koegle in the presence of the chairman and secretary of the meeting.

Judge Shay, who was our spokesman, was one of the nearest to Snevely when he drew his cannon, and the worry and excitement has so unbalanced him that we fear he has lost his mind completely, but the doctor thinks it is only temporary. We have to watch him night and day, not knowing what turn he may take. Shay is well liked by all in Eagle, and this makes it all the worse for Snevely.

The people here are wide awake and usually good people and do not believe in such rascality as is usually seen in mining camps.

Well, we have plenty of claims in good territory, but as yet, are not sure how any of them will pay, but feel confident that we shall find some of them good.[54]

Del Deyo

P.S. ---We are going to take a snapshot of the revolver Snevely drew on the boys and have it put in the show windows of Sandusky so people can see what kind of man Snevely is.

SNEVELY TELEGRAPHS THAT HE WILL ARRIVE SUNDAY

Captain J.E. Snevely, who was recently ordered out of Alaska by a miner's court, has reached the states and says he is coming to Sandusky. Seattle, Wash. papers of the 13th instant record his arrival.

---

[54] Snevely Deposed, *Sandusky Daily Register,* 19 January 1899

Yesterday, says this morning's Sandusky Register, Mr. John C. Scheufler received a telegram from Captain Snevely, dated at Council Bluffs, Ia., saying that he expected to reach Sandusky Sunday.

From *Saturday's Sandusky Journal*:

J.E. Snevely, captain of the Sandusky Klondike party, arrived home this morning, coming over the L.S. & M.S. He went direct to his home in the brick block, West Adams Street. Mr. Snevely gives it out that he is not ready to talk for publication today but may make a statement to the public early next week. He said that he knew nothing of the publication of the charges against him here; that he is very busy, and that both he and his family are naturally much excited over what has been published about his administration of the Co-Operative Mining company at Eagle City.

Mr. Snevely claims that he can account for every cent of company money in his possession and will shortly make an explanation of other matters.

The Seattle Post Intelligence, of January 13, published this story:

Captain J.E. Snevely, manager of the Alaska Co-operative Mining company of Eagle City, on the Yukon, was a passenger on the Cottage City, arriving from the north last night. He will go to his home in Sandusky, Ohio, to arrange for returning to Alaska in the spring with more men and supplies.

Capt. J. E. Snevely, who left here last February with a part of Sanduskians for the newly discovered Alaska gold fields, returned Saturday morning. He came on business connected with the Alaska Co-operative Mining Company., of which he was manager, and just as soon as certain matters, in which he is directly interested, are settled, he will immediately return. Captain Snevely looks well. A representative of The Register called upon him last evening at his home on West Adams Street for the purpose of securing an interview regarding the sensational reports printed in the local press, in which the name of Captain Snevely figured prominently. Captain Snevely talked freely about the trip from Sandusky to Alaska, but refused to be interviewed for publication in regard to some of the charges placed against him by members of the party, and whose letters have already been published. He talked with the reporter about the accusations and said that he did not want to be quoted. Captain Snevely stated that what has been printed concerning his actions while in charge of the gold seekers he knows nothing about, and after he had made a careful examination he would give out a statement. Captain Snevely proposes to tell his side of the story and will shortly give to the public the facts. He will meet with the board of directors in a few days when the matter will be investigated. Mr. Snevely will have some interesting information to present when he tells his story.

The Skagway-Atlin Budget of Jan.3 contained the following account of Mr. Snevely's trip over the ice and snow from Dawson:

Capt. J.E. Snevely, manager of the Alaska Co-operative Mining Company, arrived in town from Dawson late Saturday evening. The captain made the trip out light, bring but his blankets with him, depending on the roadhouses for shelter and sustenance. He said he found all the conveniences that could be expected, and rather enjoyed the journey, laying over several days at various points.

His company was organized at Sandusky, O. and is a closed corporation, with nothing to sell and no schemes to float. They have 20 men employed on their properties at present, each one a shareholder in the enterprise to the amount of $300.

Their holdings are distributed among the following localities: Star Gulch, Smith's Gulch, Cuban Ravine, Buckeye, Castalia, and

Last Chance creeks, in the vicinity of Eagle City. They also have a number of tributaries of Forty Mile River, some 100 in all. Many of these have been prospected and so far as their work has been prosecuted, they all promise well.

Capt. Snevely is going below for the purpose of bringing in another year's supplies for his associates. He was found engaged in drafting a map of the country about Eagle City, which interested the reporter greatly. The captain spoke enthusiastically of the possibilities of this section, giving many points of information that our readers will no doubt appreciate. Some four years ago miners by the names of Russell, Powers, Fitzgerald and Olso crossed the boundary, went up Boundary creek some eight miles, where they discovered sufficient gold to warrant the putting in of sluice boxes. High water interfered with their operations, and they crossed the divide to what is now known as Discovery Fork of American creek from this beginning the territory, extending some 100 miles square attracted attention and today it is known as a most promising gold bearing district.

At present the number of miners engaged in work or prospecting this immense district are distributed according to Mr. Snevely's estimates: Seventy Mile River 1000 men; Forty Mile, 2000, and on creeks in the immediate vicinity of Eagle City perhaps 2000 more.

The entire country, it may be said, is in American territory, and though talking modestly the captain predicts a great future for it.

Speaking of it from an agricultural point of view he says all the hardy vegetables are produced with little care, and he has seen oats shoulder high fully matured on an island in the Yukon near Eagle City.

Personal observation in many sections of Alaska will bear his statements out in this respect. Eagle City was located Feb.2, 1898, at the junction of Mission Creek and the Yukon River, 105 miles below Dawson City in American territory. The present site occupies some 80 acres, and the improvements are about 400 cabins, sheltering from 1500 to 2000 inhabitants.

The entire district is tributary to Eagle City; hence its future will be watched with interest. Referring to the lynching Mr. Snevely said he could neither deny nor affirm, but as to the other matters discussed in our local papers during the past week, he states that Mr. Cody, it was supposed, was connected with the Eagle City Mining and Development company, but the connection was not certain. The company was formed, no doubt, for the purpose of floating wild oat schemes, but Mr. Cody's absence at the period referred to was not due to any request, but Caruthers, Hall and Smith were notified to leave and won't.

Mr. Snevely's map (Appendix C), which by the way, he is making for Surveyor General Diston, shows a perfect network of creeks, on which, almost without exception, discoveries have been made. An item of interest may be looked for at any time from that section of the country.[55]

---

[55] J.E. Snevely Home, *Sandusky Daily Register,* 22 January 1899

Back to Work

Letter from Jay Livengood:

Eagle City, Alaska,   Dec.15, 1898

Dear Mother:

I have had no letters from home in some months, although I have written several. Perhaps you have not received them, so I will write a few more lines for fear you did not get any of them. I know that you write the same as I do, and I do not get them.

The mail came from Dawson and I received one from Dod Patch that was sent to Skaguay and then sent to Bennett and then sent to Dawson, then to Eagle.

The postmaster told some of our boys that the United States mail will get down here in the course of three weeks. It has been stuck at Thirty Mile River, which is not frozen over yet.

Since our little time with Snevely, things have gone along smoothly, and little Judge Shay is getting along all right again. Our boys are feeling good now and are working hard. Our new manager, Koegle, is as nice a man to my notion as one can get aquatinted with.

Charles Smith and I have just had a long, hard trip over the hills to a stream called Champion creek that is thirty miles long, and claims staked from one end to the other, but we got one claim near to Discovery, and at Discovery a man washed out of twelve pans of dirt from the surface, $19. It is the best looking stream in this district today.

We went after a bear that Deyo and R.C.L. had in a hole, but when we got there the hole was empty, so we had our chase for nothing.

Tomorrow we start for Cuban, next morning go on with our work again and in a few weeks Charlie and I will go over the hills again, a distance of about sixty miles, to a stream called Bear that looks very good. Let an Erie County boy take 300 pounds on his back and make a sixty mile trip on your roads and he would call it pretty hard sledding---but we don't mind it a little bit in four feet of snow, going up over the mountains and down again, camping in the snow, the wind sometimes blowing a gale and the weather very cold. The coldest it has been yet is 71 degrees below zero. One day last week it sprinkled a little, but it soon went back to 20 below.

There is a great lot of work going on in this section, hundreds of claims are being prospected and if there are any good strikes made around here Eagle will take a boom. It is growing fast.

Well, mother, how are the boys and all of you this winter? What is little Len doing? If he was out here with his engine, he would hardly get it steamed up before he would have to quit and go home.

It does not get light here till nearly 10 a.m. and dark again at 3p.m. You see that we have plenty of time to sleep. This is a great country to go from one extreme to another.

Now I must say good-bye. Give my best to all and write soon

Your son,

Jay Livengood[56]

---

[56] Letter from the Klondike, *Norwalk Daily Reflector,* 17 February 1899

The latest news from the Klondike was received Monday by John F. McCrystal of Sandusky. A letter arrived dated January 1st from his brother, Patrick McCrystal, who is with the Sandusky party. It was entirely of a private nature and conveyed news that all of the party were in usual health. Judge Shay is still insane, his condition being about the same. With this exception the party is in good condition and spirits and is doing well.

Mr. McCrystal stated that none of the boys had received any word from home since September 24th, and all were very anxious for the mail to get through.

Two or three late letters from members of the Sandusky-Klondike party have just been received in Sandusky. Among them is one from Howard Huntington, and another from Patrick McCrystal, the letter being dated February 26th.

The letters are generally of a personal nature, but from them the information is gleaned that Judge Shay's mental condition is unimproved. Geo. Miller, whose right collar bone was broken, was improving, and before this he has probably gone back to work.

The party is divided up, and the boys are prospecting at various places. The winter has been an exceptionally hard one for mining, the holes sunk constantly filling up with water.

When the letters were written, no tests had been made to determine whether a pay streak had been struck.

Mr. Sheppard, the messenger who went from Toledo with the letters and packets for the Sanduskians, had not reached them when the letters were mailed.[57]

Cuban Ravine   January 1, 1899

-----As this is New Year, and Sunday too, I thought I would write and tell you how we are all getting along, and what we had good for dinner. Here is our bill of fare: In the meat line we had a variety--- bacon, rabbit, grouse and fish, prune pie with bacon grease for shortening, which was out of sight in less time than it takes to write it. We also had coffee and bread. I have made up my mind to wait until next Christmas before I will be able to take dinner with you, and then I may be able to give you a Christmas present---one worth having--- as I could not send you one this Christmas. Our 19 boys are well and in the best of health, but little Judge Shay is as crazy as a loon. I have my doubts if he ever gets any better. Some say crazy people are affected by the changes of the moon. We will soon find out, as the moon will soon change. The boys are all hard at work. I am still on Cuban Ravine punching down a few holes. The water has been bothering us a good deal this winter. We get down 19 or 20 feet, then the water will come in and fill the hole full, so we haven't made the greatest headway so far. The water will soon stop. We are sinking about two miles from camp, and the water is about dried up, so I don't think we will have any trouble in that line. We will soon be to bed rock, then we will know whether we will have a pay streak or not. We are scattered around over a good lot of ground and doing

---

[57] Klondike Boys are Well, *Norwalk Daily Reflector,* 28 February 1899

lots of work. We ought to strike gold somewhere. The 7th day of August will tell the tale.

We have a cabin and 40 lots in Eagle that are worth $8,000 or $10,000, and there are some people who want to get hold of them now; but we will hold on to them until next summer, when we think Eagle will take quite a boom, for there is lots of work being done on every stream within 60 miles of Eagle. People are leaving Dawson quite lively.

It is estimated there will be 10,000 people go out over the ice. The weather has been quite mild the past week---about 30 to 40 below zero. The wind has been blowing a gale and snow has been drifting, making it hard traveling going to and from work.

January 22

----Well, mother, now I will try and finish my letter. Yesterday I left Cuban and came to Eagle where I found several letters for me. They were dated June and July. One from Eva B. was mailed as late as May 18, one of yours was May 18, one July 13, and one July28; one from Bertha, May 18, and one with nothing but envelopes in it, but nothing in it to tell who it was from. One of yours had ten 5-cent stamps in it, which will come in just right now, as I did not have a stamp and you cannot buy one at Eagle at any price. The weather is nice and not very cold. It runs from 20 degrees to 60 degrees below zero. Everybody is out in the hills sinking holes. I haven't heard of any big strike yet. In some places the water has hindered the people in prospecting. It has bothered us a great deal, but in February it will stop some of our boys are getting quite homesick, but as for myself, I cannot complain as long as I know you are all well at home.

Ross and I started out after two moose the other day. We started them in Cuban and followed them over the summit into the Boundary. We had a hot old chase. We followed them until after 8 o'clock that night. We got in the next day at noon, hungry and tired.

February 3

Well, mother, there hasn't been any mail in yet. Pat came up from Eagle today and said the mail had not come in, but a lot of reindeer had just gone down from Dawson to Circle for the government. They camped at Eagle R.R., and a wolf killed one of them night before last. Pat brought me a letter from Vin that was mailed September 18 and was the first one I have received from him since July. There is not much use of writing, for the mail won't go out until the ice moves off the Yukon. As I am still at Cuban I don't see or hear much. I see Indians as they pass through; three of them stopped for dinner with us the other day. They told us to stop when we go to Eagle, and they will give us some moose meat for a change. We spend the long evenings playing cribbage after we get our supper and work done. You can tell Frank McGill I will give him a whirl at 13 to 1 when I get back to old Ohio.

Jay Livengood[58]

---

[58] A Letter from Alaska, *Norwalk Daily Reflector,* 6 April 1899

The Kings of Slate Creek

From the *Sandusky Register:*

"Encouraging news regarding the Sandusky party now in Alaska has been received in this city. The information at hand is to the effect that the gold hunters have struck 'pay dirt', and that each man now on the ground will be able to reap the reward, in a financial way, of many months of hard work in the land of snow and ice. H.C.Huntington received a letter on Tuesday from his son, Howard R. Huntington, who furnishes the good news to Sanduskians". The following is an extract from Mr. Huntington's letter:

A pay streak of about 60 feet in width and three feet deep, lying on a bed rock only six feet from the ground surface, has shown all the way from 10 cents to 40 cents to the pan, and under favorable conditions that means a creek that will pay nearly $30.00 per day to the man. The mouth of the creek is 40 miles from Eagle and the claims showing the above results are from 15 to 25 miles up the creek. Many of the pups or tributaries to Slate have been staked and prospected, and some have shown very good colors. There is every reason to believe, if any credit is to be placed in the opinions of the old miners, that the whole Slate creek district is rich, both in its bed and in the benches lining it. You have no idea what effect a report of this kind has on a mining community. Two months ago we sent a man (Deacon Widman) over there on the strength of a rumor started by parties that had been in that country last summer. He got there several weeks before the real rush and stampede began from Eagle and secured some of the property on the creek. Since that time we have hauled him provisions enough so that he could stay and thoroughly prospect the creek. He sunk 13 holes in company with several parties owning the adjoining claims and it was in these holes that the find was made. Meanwhile three more of our party had been over there and staked on several of the main pups. They are all back now and the Buckeye cabin has become a sort of information bureau for slate creek. For two weeks before Deacon returned, reports of wealth varying from 30 cents to $2 to the pan were circulated, but all were waiting for Deacon to have them verified or disputed. Men came to our cabin day after day always inquiring for news of Slate and the whereabouts of our prospectors. Now that they have returned and well-founded story has been given out, there has commenced an exodus from Eagle that may empty the town of all but woman and children for a few days. A sample of Slate creek gold was very carefully packed and brought over here in Armours extract of beef can, and when tested at N.A.T. & A. Co.'s store downtown, in the presence of many interested and anxious miners, resulted in a showing of 35 cents to the pan. This was from one of our claims, and though the average may not give so much as that, it is enough to insure good diggings. Slate creek is wide, perhaps too much so for ordinary ground sluicing, and it will take several months of summer to get a claim in shape to take out pay, but there are many slower ways of working, such as rocking the gravel, that will be used there next summer and will give many miners something more than his winter outfit. In spite of the hardships of the trail and the severe cold we are having now, several women have gone to Slate, some pulling their own sleds and others going in a party as cooks. The trail is in bad shape.[59]

Howard

The late mail from Alaska brought a large number of letters from the Sandusky party, telling their friends of their good luck in discovering gold along Slate creek. Among the letters received is the following from Jay Livengood.

Eagle City, Alaska   March 1, 1899

Dear Mother:

I have just got back from a trip to Slate creek, way over in the Forty Mile district where we have quite a number of claims and good ones too. We can get from 13 to 33 cents per pan. It is nearly a hundred miles away. We will commence to get our grub over right away so as to begin work at once. It is only from four to six feet to bed rock and the pay streak is from one to two feet deep. The boys are all feeling good over our find. We had a cold trip going over and coming back. Widman had been over prospecting for a long time and Frank G. Minzer and Frank Way and myself followed. We were out twelve days going and coming. Pushing your sled for a hundred miles and back and breaking trail over the mountains in deep snow is not like sitting in a cutter behind a good horse going to Sandusky.

---

[59] Picking Up Gold, The Sandusky-Klondike Party Has Found Paying Claims, *Norwalk Daily Reflector,* 7 April 1899

Two of the boys froze their feet. I frosted[60] my nose and one ear. We are feeling good after our long trip. I just received five letters, three from you and two from Vin. I will write you a longer letter in a few days. So goodbye.

From your son.

Jay

From the *Sandusky Journal:*

"Mr. and Mrs. H.C. Huntington have just received two letters from their son Howard R. Huntington, dated at Eagle City, Alaska, March 9th. In Mr. Huntington's letter, pertaining principally to business matters, Howard writes with regard to latest information concerning their claims on Slate Creek, that a mining expert estimates the value of the claim already opened at $250,000 and bases his estimates on an average of 13 cents per pan. As stated in a previous letter, a test proved that some of the pans yielded 35 cents".

Extracts from the letter to Mrs. Huntington are as follows:

Eagle City, Alaska   March 9, 1899

My Dear Mother:

Another opportunity to send out mail, and this time by a couple of Princeton graduates, who are on their way to the states. You see

---

[60] Gold Seekers Rich Find, *Norwalk Daily Reflector,* 10 April 1899

I miss no chance of letting you hear from me. It is some time since I have written you, so most of my late letters have been largely composed of business matters and addressed to father. And now let me caution you against one thing. If you receive no letters from me during the next few months, don't worry. I shall be in the back woods all summer, and in fact from now on. Seventy miles from town and the only means of transportation is aboard Shank's mare. I will do my best to get letters in from the creek, but it probably won't be often.

We are in good shape to go out there; have plenty of good food---better than we have had at any time before---and the party is considerably encouraged over our prospect in the new district.

I hope next September will see us all supplied with a little sock full of the yellow. Speaking of socks, if you can get any very heavy woolen ones at home send me a half dozen pairs in that box, I believe you are preparing for the first boat from down the river. They are worth $2 per pair here and very few in stock, and those of poor quality. You ought to see some samples of my darning---talk about your crazy quilts and openwork knitting---why, my socks will take the prize in any county fair in Ohio. I have found a washerwoman even on this frozen soil, and she only charges 25 cents per piece. Regular rates are 50 cents. When we are on Slate Creek, however, and shoveling in gold, I am afraid washing will be a semi-annual event; once now, and once again when we return in September.

We start tomorrow morning and Thiem and I are to work together during the trip over, which will last about 40 days. We have eight dogs to help us in this work, but seven of them are only pups that can't work much yet.

Yesterday I received Father's letter of August 2d, to which I must now reply.[61]

Always Your Loving Son,

Howard

In explanation of the statement about the 40 days trip from Eagle City to Slate Creek, it may be stated that the men would likely have carried with them a summer's supply of provisions. They would almost certainly establish caches along the route, carrying a part of the load at a time to the first cache. They then would have established a second cache further along, removing the stores to it, and so on until they arrived at Slate Creek. ---(Ed.)

From the *Sandusky Journal*:

A letter just received by Mr. Huntington, from Mr. Shay, of Seattle, brings intelligence from Eagle City, under date of March 20th, eleven days later than the letter of H.R. Huntington, published in our columns last Tuesday.

Mr. Shay writes that he has just received a letter from his son Julian, which, after being subjected to closest scrutiny, does not indicate any derangement or insanity. It was a cheerful letter in which he speaks of his sickness and recovery. Young Shay says in his letter to his father that their party are now dubbed "Slate Creek Kings," and that he thinks a most excellent find has been made. "We

---

[61] A Quarter Million, *Norwalk Daily Reflector,* 20 April 1899

have purchased a most generous supply of canned vegetables and fruit and meats in addition to the usual supplies of pork and beans.' He says he is "now able to drag a sled carrying 150 pounds, eleven miles a day, and sleep well from fatigue."

Mr. Shay writes that it is hard to reconcile his letter with those received here under date of March 1st, which reported no improvement in his son's condition, but hopes and trust that his latest intelligence may prove true.[62]

From the *Sandusky Star Journal*:

Mrs. James Sanderson has received some letters from her husband in the Klondike, portions of which we are permitted to print. Owing to irregularity in the mails, some of these letters were greatly delayed. Under the date of February 22d he tells of the starting of Widman, Adelman, Livengood and Meinzer for Slate Creek, the place where later the lucky strike was made.

He writes:

March 5th

It is a common report that the Buckeye party has struck it rich, and we are being congratulated on every side. No doubt the newspapers will be filled with the discovery of other parts in Slate Creek. We have succeeded in getting 12 claims over there and Widman prospected two of them. He found 35 cents to the pan in the 13 holes he put down six feet to bed rock. The pay streak is from

---

[62] Slate Creek Kings, *Norwalk Daily Reflector,* 25 April 1899

50 to 60 feet wide and three feet deep, all summer diggings, with plenty of water for sluicing.

The United States Surveyor here estimated the two claims as worth $500,000. We are all going over there at once. We will get started sometime next week. The N.A.T. & T. Company has trusted us to $1,000 worth of provisions to complete our summer outfit. All the boys are moving in from the different claims where they have been at work during the winter. We will hold them over and let someone else prospect them for us. We got down five feet on Welch Pup but had not reached bed rock when called off. No pay dirt was found, although the place seemed to be fine. We have not given up hopes yet Last week Henry Zurcher and I went up and brought back a large load of digging tools, etc. We got back just at dusk, two very tired and hungry men. It was between 50 and 60 below. Most people will not go out when it is below 40 but I do not mind it. The little bottles of mercury had frozen solid, as had our tobacco. We could not cut that with a knife.

Quite a number have been frozen this winter. One man at Dawson was found dead with a stick in one hand and his knife in the other, frozen in the act of lighting a fire. Another man froze both of his hands so badly that he will lose them. He was within half a mile of shelter and did not know it.

March 12

The man that froze his hands had them amputated here in Eagle yesterday. Poor fellow, he is worse off than the man who died. Willie Fettle froze both his feet about three weeks ago in the Cuban Ravine. We got a doctor for him and he'll be back at work this week.

I suppose this will be my last Sunday in the cabin on the Yukon. We have had pleasant times here and regret to leave.

We commenced to move last Thursday. We travel in pairs. Charlie Koegle and I work together. Each took 250 pounds 13 miles up Mission River and pitched a camp. There we left six men and eight dogs. They will move it 12 miles up the river to the mouth of Clifford creek. The rest of us returned and made a round trip Friday and Saturday. We have never done any work on Sunday unless it was necessary, besides when a man makes 20 miles a day in this climate he does not have to be asked to rest on Sunday. We will get all our supplies over to Eagle this week and then we will be on the trail again, living in tents and sleeping on the snow. We now have six tons to move, and it is 70 miles to our first claim. Widman and Gleckner will push 30 miles further and prospect two claims on Ruby Creek before the thaw comes. Good reports are coming from Ruby Creek and we are anxious to know what we have got there. The Judge is feeling pretty good physically but can do no work. We will take him with us. Dell Deyo is cook.

James Sanderson

Mr. Sanderson also gave much information concerning the price of provisions. Prices kept up in everything except flour, which is $16 a hundred. Additionally, they are having a "Whisky War", and the price has been reduced to 25 cents a drink.

Reportedly he felt very much encouraged over the prospects, and sure that the Buckeye party had some rich holdings that would prove of immense value. The company now had property on Slate Creek, Ruby Creek, and in Eagle, and the most conservative estimate of its value would be far beyond the mildest expectations of the most sanguine before they started.

The summer season had by this time opened, and in all probability the Klondike party would soon be reaping a rich harvest from their claims.[63] A special to the *Cincinnati Inquirer* dated Dawson, Alaska, via San Francisco, says:

The winters work on the Klondike claims has been generally satisfactory to the industrious. Nineteen or more Ohioans have shared in the generally profitable clean-up. They have locations on Slate creek, which enters Eureka creek at Discovery. The Discovery is 20 miles from the mouth, and from the mouth to 43 miles above, the creek is staked and recorded. Prospect holes have been sunk at frequent intervals over this long stretch and in no instance without finding coarse gold. The creek is said to have developed not a single "knocker" out of all the crowds who have stampeded in this last winter.

The creek was staked originally about July 4th and the tributary was also thoroughly staked. It comes in near Discovery and is named Fourth of July.

There are now about 50 men at work on the creek, and 20 well separated claims. Many others are engaged in taking provisions over, for diggings are all shallow. Real work will be done this summer. A party of 19, known as the Buckeye boys, who own several claims, have thoroughly prospected No. 13 below and for a width across the creek of 30 feet. They find a depth of three feet of gravel

---

[63] From The Klondike, *Norwalk Daily Reflector,* 6 May 1899

which pans from 6 to 40 cents. Bed rock is 8 feet deep with 3 feet of snow.

The Buckeye boys are Charles Koegle, manager; Sylvester Widman, James Sanderson, George Gleckner, William Thiem, William Fettle, Howard Huntington, George Miller, Chas. Smith, Abe Meinzer, Henry Zurcher, William Cohen, J.L. and Ross Livengood, Frank Adelman, Dell Deyo and Patrick McCrystal all of Sandusky, and Julian J.Shay and Perry Hutchens of Dayton. They form the Alaska Co-Operative Mining Company Corporation, formed at Sandusky and of which J.E.Snevely was manager. The company owns 12 claims in the vicinity.[64]

From the *Sandusky Star Journal*:

There is an exciting long distance race on between H.C.Huntington and J.E.Snevely, the goal being Eagle City, Alaska. Across ten states, out upon the Pacific Ocean across the trails of wild Alaska and down the great Yukon's swirling rapids and treacherous channels these two men will hurry as fast as steam, beasts, shank's horses" or any other mode of transportation will carry them. Mr. Huntington's mission is well known. He carries messages of love and greeting from friends in Ohio to the Sandusky party in the gold fields. He takes many packages containing some little token, some comfort from home to these men who are practically exiled from civilization for the time being. The most important object, however, is to take inventory of the claims of the property of the Alaska Co-Operative Mining company, and to make

---

[64] The Buckeye Boys, *Norwalk Daily Reflector,* 29 May 1899

arrangements for a continuance of the work so laboriously begun, and of which now promises to be productive of rich results.

The object of Snevely's trip can only be conjectured. The theory has been advanced, however, that either by bluff, apology for past misconduct, or by some other means, it is his intention to join the Sandusky gold hunters. Last Monday a certain local stockholder of the Alaska Co-Operative Mining company received a telegram from another stockholder at Seattle Wash., saying that Snevely was there, registered at the Butler House, and that he would sail the next day (Tuesday) for Alaska. A draft for $500, made by Snevely upon the mining company has also been received here by one of the banks, but was not cashed. From the fact that Snevely drew upon the company, it is supposed that he still considers himself an employ, under his contract which does not expire until August. The company, it will be remembered, ousted him some time ago on account of his alleged mismanagement, and it is understood that it has since refused to pay him any longer. The question as to whether Snevely's contract with the company is still in effect, despite the action of the board of directors, may result in some interesting complications and possibly a lawsuit. It is understood that there were six important letters sent by J.C.Scheufler, secretary, and addressed to "Capt. J.E.Snevely, manager of the A.C.M. Co., Eagle City, Alaska." It is supposed that these letters are still held in the Eagle City post office, and one reason for the race to Alaska between Mr. Huntington and Snevely, will be to get possession of them. The claim will be set up that

Snevely, being no longer manager of the company, is not entitled to them, as they are addressed not to him personally, but in his official capacity.

Snevely, it is understood, is armed with a commission as notary public for Eagle City from the provincial government of Alaska. He also took with him a surveyor's outfit. Just how he expects to make use of these things is not known, but a significant fact in this connection is that the claims of the Co-Operative Mining company in Alaska were taken in the name of J.E.Snevely, manager.

Mr. Huntington, it will be remembered, Left Sandusky last Wednesday at midnight. He remained over Thursday in Chicago and should arrive in Seattle today. Provided he can immediately take ship for Alaska, Snevely will still have five days the start of him. Transportation in Alaska is still a very uncertain quantify, however, and it is still possible that Mr. Huntington may overtake Snevely at Lake Bennett before the latter can take passage on a boat down the Yukon.[65]

From the *Sandusky Register*:

The first letters from the Klondike to reach here for several weeks arrived yesterday morning. Letters were received from Howard Huntington, George J.Miller, Charles Koegle and a number of others. They are of widely differing dates, the earlier written ones having evidently been delayed somewhere. The latest letters were written in April, one being dated the 23rd.

All of the letters express a very hopeful feeling. The party had just reached its new claims on Slate creek at the time the latest letters were written, and the work started. Prospects were excellent, but nothing definite could be given in the letters written, as but

---

[65] Race For Klondike, *Norwalk Daily Reflector,* 9 June 1899

little progress had been made. The trip to Slate Cut was a laborious one, and the men were greatly relieved when they had covered the 80 miles.

The party is somewhat crippled, a number of the men being laid up by accident or by disease. George J. Miller has been the most unfortunate. He has suffered from a broken collar bone, frozen feet, frozen ears, and had one finger amputated. His latest misfortune was a shot wound. Mr. Howard in an interesting letter gives the following account of the accident: "In the move up from Clifford to the summit, where ptarmigan were thick, Cowen and Miller were working on the same sled. Cowan had his gun (probably cocked) in the case, and in an attempt to pull it out to shoot at a bird, the trigger caught and the gun went off, discharging most of the load into Millers hip, but near the outside of the leg, so that no bones were touched and the injury not great. He was taken at once to Eagle and put under a doctor's care and into a good cabin, where he will be well nursed.

Poor Cowan was terribly upset over it. Miller will be around in a couple of weeks though, as the wound is healing well. Shay is doing good work on the trail; is rational most of the time. Talk about Snevely is enough to upset him at any moment. He will probably be sent out early in the summer.

In addition to Miller and Shay, Dell Deyo is also in bad shape, suffering from rheumatism and scurvy. He was hauled to Eagle City by Koegle and Huntington and placed under the care of a physician. He will probably be sent home this summer. Miller also expects to come home if possible.

Mr. H.C.Huntington, who is on his way to Slate creek, as the representative of the company, has probably nearly reached his destination. Upon his arrival there, more definite arrangements will be made for the future.[66]

George J Miller, the first to return of the party of Sandusky men who went to Alaska in search of gold, arrived in the city Saturday afternoon at 5:54 coming directly from Chicago. He did not bring any gold with him, but he gives a good report of the conditions there and is enthusiastic over the prospects of the Sandusky company.

Mr. Miller was very tired when seen by a Register man yesterday and did not care to talk much. He had arrived here after a journey of nearly 9,000 miles and then did not get much sleep. Many of his friends called to welcome him home, and when he did retire, he did not sleep because, as he said, the bed was too soft. After 18 months of rough camp life, a good bed was too much of a luxury.

Mr. Miller told the Register man the same story he had told to many people during the day. He appeared to be in good health, though it was evident that his left leg, which was shot, still bothered him. He walks with a limp. He said that it was pretty well healed, except below the knee, where all of the trouble seemed to have located, and the wound will require long and careful treatment. With the exception of the leg, Mr. Miller is enjoying good health.

Mr. Miller, after he was wounded was removed to Eagle City, and later was taken to Circle City, where he was placed in a hospital. The treatment there however, afforded him no relief, and he was told that he must return to the states. After being in the hospital for

---

[66] In Camp at Slate Creek, *Norwalk Daily Reflector,* 29 June 1899

two weeks he left on July 8 for home. He was accompanied by Dell Deyo, who was suffering from scurvy. They went to St. Michael's and there sailed for San Francisco where they arrived safely, and both improved in health. Mr. Miller went to Seattle and Mr. Deyo to Astoria, where he will remain for some time. Deyo improved rapidly and was able to walk around without the use of a cane when he left San Francisco. He will probably return home after fully recovering in the invigorating western climate.

Mr. Miller came from Seattle to Chicago and thence to Sandusky, making in all a trip of nearly 9,000 miles, occupying in all about 36 days. The trip was a long and tiring one and Mr. Miller was naturally glad to reach home and get some much needed rest

Asked as to the prospects of the Sandusky party for securing gold, Mr. Miller did not care to say much, except to express great confidence in the result of the work. He said he was very anxious to return if his leg would heal up so as to allow him. He said that he learned from relatives of Judge Shay at Seattle that the dam that was constructed at great labor by the Sandusky men on Slate creek had burst, causing considerable delay and extra work. However, he did not know how true the report was as he left before any news of the disaster had reached him. Being at Eagle City and Circle City for some time, he had not seen the rest of the party and some letters that reached here before he did contained news for him.

He saw Mr. Huntington at Eagle but did not know what arrangements were made with the men. Mr. Miller said he thought most of the men would return to the states with Mr. Huntington, who has probably left by this time. He did not care to say anything about the affair with Captain Snevely, saying that he would await the return of Mr. Huntington. Mr. Miller had not seen Snevely in

Alaska since the latter was ordered out, though it was reported that Mr. Huntington had seen him.

Mr. Miller talked entertainingly, and his reminiscences would fill a good sized newspaper. He has a complete diary of the events since the party left Sandusky on Feb. 7, 18 months ago, and will be able to give some interesting stories of the camp.[67]

The following letter was received from J.E. Snevely was in Alaska:

Eagle City, Alaska   July 10, 1899

Ed. Register

In compliance with your request and my promise to write you, before I left Sandusky, I now take pleasure in saying that I arrived here safely after a pleasant journey and some delay by reason of having stopped at Muir Glacier for three weeks to prospect and locate a quartz claim which I discovered while enroute to Sitka and of which I will give full details later.

I found many friends here glad to see me back, but on account of the stampede to Cape Nome, Eagle City seems quite deserted. As our Sandusky people are more interested in the Buckeye boys than anything else, I will tell you of them first. From the best information obtainable, Mr. H.C. Huntington arrived here about three weeks ago. He found Koegle awaiting him after a wait (for unknown reason) of ten or twelve days. He and Koegle made the trip over to

---

[67] Returned From Alaska, *Sandusky Register,* 14 August 1899

Slate Creek, but three or four days before they arrived the dam across Slate Creek, on which the boys say, five or ten thousand dollars' worth of labor had been expended, had washed out and was entirely destroyed, so by the time Mr. Huntington arrived on the ground the boys were all ready for a meeting, which was held, and a decision reached to return everything to Eagle. So ended the Slate Creek exploit.

On one of the trips in, George Miller was accidentally shot in the groin with a load of buckshot and very narrowly escaped a mortal wound. Miller has undoubtedly been the most unfortunate of all the Sandusky party to the Klondike, except perhaps Deyo who is now suffering with scurvy and rheumatism. After the party's return to Eagle, Miller and Deyo were put into a small boat and set adrift to float down the river, their destination being Circle City hospital, but if able they will no doubt, be in the states by the time this reaches you.

Mr. Huntington is working at the sawmill earning $15 per day, the balance of the party working are up on the once despised Lake Erie placer claim.

At this writing I have just received a communication that reads as follows:

Eagle City, Alaska   July 19, 1899

J.E.Snevely:

Dear Sir:

Your two letters of invitation of the stockholders
in the field of the A.C.M. Co. have been shown to me.
It must be evident that these men under advices from
Sandusky do not know of any authority vested in you
that would warrant a consultation with reference to
future plans, and I am requested by them to say that
their time is otherwise engaged. As a stockholder of
the A.C.M. Co. you have a right to know what the
plans are for future work that have been adopted by
the board of directors, and it is my duty to make them
known. If it is agreeable to you to meet me at
Cochran's cabin today. You may name the hour and
my time will be at your service.

Yours Truly,

H.C .HUNTINGTON

So that you may better understand the purport of this communication, I herewith append the following:

Eagle City, Alaska   July 17

To the members of the Buckeye Party Now in Eagle City:

Gentlemen:

I have just arrived and would be pleased to meet any member or members of the party at the N.A.T. and T. Co.'s store who desire to do so at any hour on July 18, 1899, suitable to your convenience, to talk over our business relations, and if possible to formulate plans for future operations. I can assure you that it will be to your interest to consider this proposition well and act wisely.

Yours Respectfully,

J.E.SNEVELY

Agent A.C.M. Co.

To this I sent the following making the second communication referred to in Huntington's letter above,

Eagle City, Alaska   July 18

To the Stockholders in the A.C.M. Co. now at Eagle City:

Gentlemen;---On the 17th last I had my first notification that I was not the agent of the A.C.M. Co. in view of that fact and the further fact that I am the largest stockholder of the company, I have information of importance to impart to the stockholders here, it will therefore be of vital financial interest to S. Widman, Chas. Koegle, George Gleckner, Abe Minzer, J.B. Sanderson, Pat McCrystal, Perry Hutchins, J.L. Shay, William Cowan, H. W. Zurcher, Charles Smith, Frank Adelman, William Thiem, William Fettle, J. Livengood, and R. Livengood to meet me at an early date in a conference on matters pertaining to our business in this country. This invitation is addressed to the above named gentlemen individually or collectively. I will be glad to meet them at any place or time with the next 24 hours.

Respectfully,

J.E. SNEVELY

I omitted the names of Miller and Deyo because they were not here and the name of H. R. Huntington because I have many good reasons, which I will give later, to make me believe that he, in connection with his father, were the instigators and prime movers in all the trouble I have had with the men. I have good reason also to believe that Mr. H.C. Huntington has prevented any of the men from seeing me and submitted personally the communication first mentioned above.

I will meet Mr. Huntington this afternoon and give you the result of our interview in a future letter. Will take pleasure in answering any and all questions regarding my relations with the A.C.M. Co. the city or country in general, through the columns of The Register, for which I will be a regular correspondent.

Yours Truly,

J.E. SNEVELY[68]

Jay Livengood, one of the Sandusky men in the Klondike, writes to his mother as follows:

Eagle City   July 14, 1899

Mr. Huntington is with us now but expects to leave as soon as a steamer comes from Dawson. Tomorrow C. Smith and I will commence to fish for salmon, while the other boys will be at work

---

[68] SNEVELY, *Sandusky Daily Register,* 16 August 1899

on the Lake Erie placer claim sluicing to see just what is in it until our time is up with the company. We just came in from Slate creek by way of Forty Mile Creek, a distance of 200 miles. There were thirteen of our boys and one man by the name of Bryan. He has the scurvy and could not walk. We had a nice trip and saw lots of country. It is a great mining country, and they take out lots of gold. Mr. Huntington wanted to go along with us, but we thought it would not be best on account of the danger of being swamped and someone getting hurt, for we were told it was a very dangerous river to run; but we made it all right and the sick man did not get wet a bit. But the rest of us were not dry from the time we started. We were in the water every day and in some places the boys had to swim. We went through some pretty bad places.

I think I will have to stay in Alaska one more winter and see just what I can do. As our dam went out we did not get to taking out any of the dust, so we are all shy on our expectations. I do not look for anything this year. We all signed the new contract, and when someone else opens up our claim we will go to work on it again. In the present condition we could do nothing, as it takes money to open up a claim and that article is just a little short with us now. I was in hopes of getting a little out of Slate Creek, but we may have better luck in Lake Erie.

My clothes are a little the worse for wear, but then as long as I can get canvas sacks I can make them do. I think I shall come back with the tailor trade well learned, and when I get back home I can do my own washing and mending.

Well, on the Fourth of July Capt. Koegle brought me four letters. I was so glad to get them, for I had worried so much, thinking perhaps some of you had caught that awful smallpox. One letter was dated April 28, with Canada stamps in. I thank you very much for them, as they will come in handy this winter to get letters out to you. Well mother, I don't know what will interest you, so I think I will quit and write oftener in the future than I have been doing in the last few months, for I am where I can mail them if I write. So good-bye, and don't look for me this winter, but after this winter will meet with the boys at Parker's store

Your son,

Jay[69]

TIME OF THE SANDUSKY KLONDIKERS HAS EXPIRED

Mr. Jay Livengood writes the following letter from Eagle City, Alaska:

July 28.

-----I will now answer your letter received the morning Mr. Huntington left Eagle; haven't had time to answer sooner as I have been up the river fishing for salmon. It is raining, so I will not go back till morning. We are up the river from Eagle about eight miles. We are catching a few fish. I wish I could send you about a 50-pounder for your breakfast. I think it would give you salmon enough for one meal.

---

[69] Sandusky Klondikers, *Norwalk Daily Reflector,* 24 August 1899

Our time is drawing to a close, when each man can and must hustle for himself, and I am one that intends to look out for Jay. Some of the boys are anxiously waiting for the time when they can start to old Ohio and put their feet under their own table and get a good square meal for once. I would like to be one of them, but I want to try and get a claim of my own, so no one can dictate to me what I can or cannot do. I think if I can get a grub stake I may do something by staying in one more winter. I think I will get a job running the engine in the sawmill.

The soldiers are busy building their barracks.

Last night we had a meeting and straightened up our affairs, so the boys can go out on the first boat that comes along. Some of the boys have worked on some of the boats. I will get out a few logs; Frank Adelman and myself have a contract for two thousand feet for the sawmill. I think there will be lots of work around Eagle this winter; the soldiers are here and things are booming. The United States government has shipped horses and cattle, a sawmill, and also farming implements. They intend to do some farming around Eagle next summer. Eagle will be quite a place someday.

Well, mother, Ross will soon be home and can tell you more in an hour than I can put on paper in a week. I would have written a longer letter, but have not the time, as I start up the river this morning to commence my job.

Jay[70]

---

[70] Hustle for Themselves, *Sandusky Daily Register,* 8 September 1899

Coming Home

It was the third of August and the Sandusky Klondikers contract had expired. The fifteen acre lot containing the large log building had been sold to the NAT&T Co. in March, and the smaller cabin at Eagle was to be used by Koegle and Huntington who were staying behind to look after the interests of the ACM Company. The rest of the party would catch the first river steamer going back to St. Michaels the following morning.

Having packed their things in readiness for their trip home, the men gathered around a farewell campfire for the last time that night. They stared into the fire as the burning logs shot fiery sparks into the night sky, just as bright and sparkling as their expectations had been when they left Sandusky eighteen months ago. Now, like their hopes and dreams, the sparks were falling back to earth as sodden ashes. Although the men were excited because they would soon be home with their friends and families, they were also saddened that they were not able to bring back the riches that had been promised. About this time, the Norwalk Daily Reflector published the following article:

A number of letters have just been received in the city from the Sanduskians in the Klondike country. Mr. H.C.Huntington has received two letters from his son Howard, one being under date of August 11 and the other August 25. Extracts from Seattle newspapers of recent date with reference to affairs at Eagle City, have also been received and from the letters and papers much interesting information is gleaned.

Mr. Huntington writes that the Seattle-Yukon Transportation Co. has opened a trading post at Eagle, and their first cargo of 300 tons is just being unloaded.

Messers. Huntington and Koegle have completed the repairs upon the cabin they are to occupy this winter and have decorated the walls the best they could with posters and mosquito netting. We have a fine stove, writes Mr. Huntington, a regular range, and all we need is a Brussels carpet and a couple of silk curtains, then we would be swell. Smith and Meinzer have steady employment at the barracks and Widman at the sawmill.

Of our original 20, only Addkinson, Jay Livengood, Meinzer, Cowen, Smith, Sanderson, Widman, Koegle and myself are left. The others have all started for home.

Two big, warlike cannons point out over the banks of the Yukon from Eagle. They stand on a great broad plateau rising thirty feet above the stream, commanding the mighty river for several miles above and below the town. Judging from the details of the warlike preparations going on at Eagle one might imagine that the American Yukon metropolis was going to war with the British Dawson, a few miles across the line up the golden Yukon. Col. Ray commanding the American Yukon soldiery, has completed the erection of two cannon. Several salutes were fired in honor of the event. "The old timers all but jumped out of their boots." They were great, impressive, rumbling reports, and the echo back from the range back of the town sounded as loud as the report itself.

There are 150 soldiers at Eagle, and Col. Ray is pushing work as rapidly as possible on the government barracks, which are to cost $200,000. He wishes to get the men housed before winter.

The army post is beautifully situated. It is on a plateau as level as the floor, rising thirty feet above the river. They have an immense parade ground, which, indeed, occupies a portion of the town site, Col. Ray having purchased a number of the miner's cabins. The cannon fortifications command the river for some distance above and below the town, which is now a port of entry. All vessels going and coming must stop, and woe be unto the one that tries to run the blockade.

There is still another very interesting sight at Eagle just now. Tons---yes, hundreds of tons---of beer, whisky and other intoxicants are piled up on the banks of the river, having been denied admittance to British territory. The Canadian authorities are turning back, and have been for some time, all vessels carrying liquors. The arrival of several government officials, who crossed overland from Port Valdez, is reported at Eagle, and they say that Capt. Ambercrombie has driven his trail through a distance of fifty miles from the coast. The most experienced miners think well of the Eagle district. Under the most adverse conditions $250,000 was taken out during the season just closed. Next season's yield, it is predicted, will be three times that. There are about 2,000 people in the district and nearly 1,500 are engaged in mining pursuits.[71]

George Gleckner, who was a member of the Sandusky-Klondike party of gold seekers that left one year ago last winter for Alaska, has returned to his home in Sandusky County, and where he proposes to stay in the future. The Fremont News says:

---

[71] Only Nine Now Left, *Norwalk Daily Reflector,* 18 September 1899

George Gleckner, of Lindsey, who recently returned from the Klondike, was in town Saturday. Mr. Gleckner went to the Eagle Creek gold regions with the Sandusky-Klondike party, but came home without any gold. However, Mr. Gleckner is satisfied with his experience and stated to the News, that if he hadn't gone to the Klondike he never would have been satisfied. The Sandusky party had considerable bad luck, but they have some claims which they hope will pan out well. Mr. Gleckner says Sylvester Widman, of Rice township, is operating a sawmill out there and is making $15 a day. He further says that many more men leave the Klondike without gold in their clutches.

Mr. Gleckner was well nearly all of the time he was there, but will not return to the Alaskan gold fields, as he thinks Sandusky County is good enough for him. Mr. Widman will probably return home soon.[72]

From the Sandusky Register:

A letter received from Howard R. Huntington gives further particulars of the trip of the four returning Klondikers. They were thirteen days on the journey from Cape Nome and were literally packed in, the ship being loaded with returning gold seekers. William Fettle of this city, and Frank Adelman, of Norwalk, will soon

---

[72] Gold Seeker Returns, *Sandusky Register,* 18 September 1899

leave San Francisco for home, while Mr. Huntington and William Thiem will remain some time longer.[73]

FRANK ADELMAN AND HENRY ZURCHER RETURN

Frank Adelman and Henry Zurcher, who left here February 7th, 1898 for the Klondike with the Sandusky party, returned to their homes in Norwalk today. Adleman is in excellent health, but Zurcher looks rather thin, having lost twenty pounds in weight from stomach trouble.

Of the twenty members of the party which left for the north a year ago last February, eleven have returned to the states and nine have remained in Alaska. Those who remained are Ross Livengood, who was laid up at St. Michael's with a broken leg; William Cohen and Pat McCrystal, at Cape Nome; and Jay Livengood, James Sanderson, Charles Koegle, Al Minzer, Smith and Snevely at Eagle City.

Cohen, who formerly worked in the A.B. Chase factory, now has a job at Cape Nome that pays him $100 per month.

Zurcher left Eagle City August 5th and went to St.Michaels and Cape Nome, leaving the latter place October 23rd for San Francisco. Adleman Left Eagle City August 22nd and went to St. Michael's where he remained until October 15th, taking care of Ross Livengood. He then went to Cape Nome where he remained for

---

[73] Klondikers Are Coming Home, *Norwalk Daily Reflector,* 7 December 1899

three days and then started for San Francisco, where he met Zurcher, and they two journeyed together to Norwalk.

Adelman informed the Reflector this afternoon that the Sandusky Company has a number of fine claims in the Forty Mile creek and American creek districts, which are expected to become very valuable. He says that about all the good claims in the interior have been taken up, as have all the beach claims at Cape Nome. At the latter place, however there are some creek diggings open to claim.

The present winter, he predicts, will be a good one for work in the interior, as there has been a great exodus from Dawson and Eagle City to the Cape Nome district, and the days wages have gone up to a high figure.

 All of the Sandusky party feel greatly encouraged at the outlook, and Adleman says he expects to return to Alaska, but just when he does not know.[74]

From the Sandusky Register:

Three Sandusky boys who left here nearly two years ago with the Sandusky party, in search of gold in the Klondike fields, returned home Tuesday. They arrived at 2:15 over the B&O from Chicago, having come through from San Francisco by way of Denver, Salt Lake City and Chicago. They were Howard Huntington, William Fettle and William Thiem. All are in the best of health, but they have no gold, and are not anxious to return to the frozen north, at least

---

[74] Home From Klondike, *Norwalk Daily Reflector,* 24 November 1899

to search for gold. There are still a number of members of the party in the gold fields, they being Charles, Koegle, Jay Livengood, James Sanderson, Charles Smith, Abe Minzer, and S. Widman. Koegle has charge of the property of the Alaska Co-Operative Mining company, but the others are working for themselves (Appendix D).

William Fettle talked entertainingly to a Register man last evening. He said he left Eagle City on August 7, on the steamer Seattle, for St. Michael's, a distance of 1,800 miles. He had $8 in his pockets and worked his passage. From St.Michaels he soon continued his way to Cape Nome, the "newest" gold country. The distance is 100 miles, and the fare is $20.

On his arrival at Cape Nome, Fettle established himself as a contractor and builder. He at once secured work at $1.50 an hour. When he arrived there were but three frame buildings and one log cabin. When he left there were over 300 frame buildings. The population increased from less than 2,000 to over 5,000. Miners were rocking out from $10 to $100 a day on the beach. Nearly all the claims have been taken, but there promises to be a still greater rush in the coming spring.

While wages are high, it also costs much to live. Board varies from $5 to $10 a day. A serving of ham and eggs costs $2.50; coal is $150 a ton; whisky and beer sell at 50 cents a drink, and lumber is $50 to $200 a thousand. While Fettle was at Cape Nome, Howard Huntington joined him, and on October 18, they sailed for San Francisco. They went out on a rowboat to the steamer, and there met Thiem, and the three went on to San Francisco, the voyage occupying 14 days. They called themselves the "Dreibund."

They arrived at San Francisco on November 1, and after spending some time there, made their way home, stopping at several places en route. While their arrival was expected in a few days, the exact time was unknown, and they completely surprised their relatives and friends.[75]

---

[75] Home From the Klondike, *Norwalk Daily Register,* 7 December 1899

Epilogue

Sylvester Widman, who went to Alaska two years previous with the Sandusky Klondike party, arrived at Seattle on important business in connection with the construction of a new railroad in Alaska. Concerning his visit to Seattle, the Times of that city published the following story:

Mr. Widman brings news of the discovery and active development of an immense coal deposit fifty-five miles below Dawson. The Alaska Mining Company, of which Mr. Widman is the manager, has already put a large force of men at work developing the property, and according to Mr. Widman, the deposit consists of a blanket vein ten feet thick, which can be distinctly traced for over half a mile along the mountains abutting on the creek. Tests of the fuel have proved so satisfactory that the owners have determined to build a railroad ten miles long from the mouth of the creek to the mines, and Mr. Widman is now negotiating for the purchase of steel rails, locomotives and other equipment for a narrow-gauge road. The company proposes to establish coal stations at various points along the Yukon River, and Mr. Widman's purchases will include a suitable steamer and a fleet of barges for the purpose of carrying out this plan. The development of this extensive property on so large a scale should have a tendency to solve the fuel problem throughout all parts of Alaska reached by the Yukon River and its tributaries. Up to the present time the N.A.T. & T. Company has had the only working coal mine in the region, and the output has been far below the demand. The Alaska Pioneer Mining company is a Duluth corporation with a large working capital.[76]

On June 8th, 1919, the Sandusky Register published the following article, including an interview with Jay Livengood:

Jay Livengood, 426 Warren St., the only living Sanduskian having a live, progressive city named in his honor, once again has heard the of the wild in far off Alaska. In answer to the irresistible summons, he will leave today on a six month's business and prospecting trip in search of more gold.

Twenty-one years ago, Livengood with 19 other Sanduskians followed the great gold rush into Alaska, then an unexplored wilderness of the north. He experienced all the tortures and troubles of the early miners in their rush for sudden wealth. It was gold everywhere in those days. He saw 45,000 camped in Dawson during the bitter cold of the winter.

Not daunted by his hardships, Livengood stuck. Two of the others in his original party remained on the job. Charles W. Koegle is still digging away. He is making good too, and he may never return to this country.

Livengood has been back in the states five years. He has a number of claims now in the vicinity of the city that bears his name. They are under control of his partner, N.R. Hudson. In a recent letter, Hudson said the claims he was working had produced $25,000 in

---

[76] A New Railroad, *Norwalk Daily Register,* 16 February 1900

gold the past year, and it would take him 45 years with the same rate of progress he was now making to work it out.

It was after three months of hard prospecting and work more than five years ago that Livengood and Hudson hit pay dirt along a creek where the city of Livengood sprung up. They staked their claims before word of the strike spreads to the outside world. Six months after the information that another gold bearing field had been found there were 6,000 people in Livengood. That was five years ago. It has been growing constantly and is today a real live city.

The creek along which Livengood and Hudson found their strike is named Livengood. Another nearby is named Olive creek in honor of Mrs. Livengood. "I just want to sell out my claims and do a little more prospecting," is the way the Sanduskian put it yesterday when asked as to his trip back into Alaska.

"It's not like it was in '98," said the big robust healthy-looking man who with a twinkle in his blue eyes as he recalled those good old days. "Then we had but one boat running up the Alaska Rivers. It made one round trip a year. Today we have plenty of them. Prices were unheard of.

"In the old days of the rush we were compelled to pay unheard of prices for supplies. We were compelled to live lots of time on wild game and fish. Fortunately, there was plenty of both kinds of such meat."

"In those days there were no roads and few villages. Today Alaska has plenty of good roads and fine thriving cities. It is just as fine living there in the summer and it is in the winter. I like it both seasons. It is one of the greatest wild game countries in the world.

You can get plenty of sport there. A trip to Alaska is a fine thing for anybody."

Livengood does not show the strain through which he passed in the big rush of the first days in Alaska. He feels fine, he says, and only because of the life he has lived in the outdoors.

The Sanduskian has a watch chain with small pieces of natural gold worked into it, the first he succeeded in finding in Alaska. He also has a charm with a beautiful piece of raised work out of natural gold, showing a cabin and a windlass used in drawing up buckets out of the mines.

Livengood has two kinds of claims near Livengood. The city is located about 105 miles north of Fairbanks. One of them is of the placer variety and the other quartz. The placer claims are 1320 feet by 660 feet, or twenty acres and the quartz are 1500 by 600 feet.

The Sanduskian said he would not feel right unless he took up some new claims, after he had made a prospecting trip, before he returns home. He expects his partner Hudson to go with him on the journey.

This is a fine season of the year according to Livengood to go into Alaska. He will be back in Sandusky not later than the first of the coming year.[77]

---

[77] Jay Livengood Hears Alaska's Call, *Sandusky Register,* 8 June 1919

Ross Livengood was interviewed by a Sandusky Register Reporter, July 5, 1958:

With the pending statehood of Alaska, it is likely that many schoolboys will think more and more about going to what has been called "America's last frontier." It is also a dreamland for Ross Livengood, who farms near Milan and will be 84 on Sunday, but for a totally different reason---Livengood has been there.

Alaska was only a sort of stop for Livengood, though. His main interest was the Canadian Klondike and the gold to be found there in 1898. He was a member of the "Sandusky Klondikers" party, 20 men who left Sandusky on Feb. 7, 1898 in a group "off to the frigid zone." as it was recorded in the Sandusky Daily Register.

His memories are rich ones. He remembers a friend of his, Jack London, author of "Call of the Wild" and other books, as a "booze fighter who drank everything in sight." He remembers going to Skagway in March, going on the frozen trail to the Whitehorse rapids, and then riding a boat to Dawson.

The claims at Dawson were very wealthy. "Three creeks were rotten rich," he recalls. He also remembers his mistakes, saying he was too young to realize the value of buying a claim, which sold in those days for $25 and made many men millionaires.

Livengood signed up for the expedition a day before it left. There was a Milan butcher who got "cold" feet and pulled out, and Livengood jumped to take his place. The men on the expedition signed contracts to go up and search for gold for 18 months. They carried their provisions on their backs and slept in canvas tents while the outside temperature went to 85 degrees below zero. They had cedar bows put on the ever-frozen ice and camp stoves inside the tents and never felt the cold, according to Livengood. "I wouldn't have missed it for the world," he added.

He was there about the longest of any of the expedition, staying after they had left to hunt on his own. During this time, he received a broken leg and later went to Nome to work on beach diggings. After three months in the hospital he returned to seek gold and left the northland for home in July of 1900. He didn't come home rich, but, as he says, "I didn't come home C.O.D., either"

He traveled to Oklahoma and Florida, didn't like either place, and came back to Milan where he bought an 85 acre farm. At 84, he still puts in a good day's work on the land, commuting from his home in Rye Beach every day.

He is in excellent health feels good and says he doesn't see why he shouldn't live to be a hundred. "I've only had one medical checkup in my life, about six years ago," he recounts, "and they couldn't find anything wrong with me then."

Livengood said he was glad he had his adventure and was glad to be settled now. His favorite remark to persons questioning him about the Klondike after his return was "Go bump your own head; I did."[78]

---

[78] Milan Farmer Recalls Klondike Gold Rush Days, *Sandusky Register,* 5 July, 1958

Biographies

Jay Livengood- 1868-1946

Jay Harrington Livengood was my grandfather, Ross Livengood's, first cousin. They were also partners during the gold rush to the Klondike in 1898. Jay was born and raised at Sand Hill a crossroad community south of Sandusky, Ohio. He was the son of Seth and Rosannah Livengood and had three brothers. David, the oldest was usually referred to as Dee or D.T. His younger brothers were Seth Jr, and Charles. Jay's father, Seth, was a private in Co. A, Ohio 72nd G.A.R. Enlisting in 1861 he fought in the battle of Shiloh during the Civil War after which he returned to Erie County. He died in 1879 of Typhoid. After Jay's father died his mother supported the family by operating a boarding house in their home and the older boys helped out by working as a blacksmith at Sand Hill. Jay worked as a stone cutter in the limestone quarries in nearby Parkertown. Jay was one of the members of the Alaska Co-operative Mining Company that left Sandusky in 1898 to join the gold rush to the Klondike.

After the A.C.M. Co. contract expired in July of 1900, Jay and a few of the others decided to remain in Alaska and try to find gold on their own. Jay and his new partner Ted Hudson left Eagle in July of 1900 to join the stampede to the beaches of Nome where a new gold rush had begun.

Jay returned to Sandusky and married Susan Olive Doerflinger in 1908, their daughter Ruth was born the following year. Olive is a niece of Charles W. Koegle who was another member of the "Sandusky Klondikers." Jay worked as a contractor for a few years in Sandusky with his father-in-law, but Alaska kept calling him back.

He returned to Alaska in 1911 rejoining his former partner Teddy Hudson to prospect for gold once again.

There are several accounts of how the two prospectors happened to travel to the Tolovana River to prospect on the spring of 1914. Richard Hudson is a grandson of Ted Hudson and the son of Clifton W. Hudson, Richard said that Jay and Ted were dead broke with winter coming on in 1913. They were in dire straits, so they decided to winter over with some Minto Indians. Richard said that the Indians told them about having seen gold on the Tolovana River. The following spring, grubstaked by C.W. Hudson, they headed for the Tolovana, bringing Hudson's brother Jim along. Ted Hudson and Jay Livengood loaded up pack horses and Jim Hudson loaded a boat with supplies. Jim planned to travel up the Tolovana River and rendezvous with them.[79]

Edwin "Eddy" Hudson, Ted's nephew, who came to Livengood in 1922, said "Jim never did make it to Livengood camp until after the stampede. His boat got hung up on at Logjam. Ted and Jay found some bedrock sticking out on what was to be Ruth Creek. They panned there and got a really nice prospect of gold". Alaska Magazine reported "Hudson and Livengood had prospected earlier in Nome, where they found a streak of gold embedded in ice. Thinking that they were going to strike it rich they christened the place "Hudsonville", after Ted Hudson. Two years later the streak ran out and they were broke." Jay wanted to again name their new discovery Hudson. But Ted said 'No, we've already had one Hudson

---

[79] Telephone Interview with Richard Hudson of Ester Alaska, 27 July 2003

that went broke,' so they named the new strike after Jay, and that was the beginning of Livengood."[80]

The Livengood camp proved a success. More than 400,000 ounces of gold, worth about $180 million at 1987 prices, has been sluiced from the ground by the stampede of miners that followed Ted and Jay. Their discovery was the last major gold strike in Alaska. Their claims were on Livengood Creek a tributary of the Tolovana River. The town of Livengood was established when miners flocked into the area upon hearing news of the strike. According to Ed Ferrell who wrote an article for Alaska Sportsman, Oct 1967 edition, "By 1916, Livengood was a prosperous camp with a population of 250 people, of whom 48 were woman. The town boasted: five outfitting stores, two saloons, one roadhouse and saloon, three restaurants, three boarding houses, one sheet metal shop, one butcher shop, one doctor, one dentist, two blacksmiths, four barber shops, one cigar store and a three-piece band. The Livengood area has produced 9 1/2 million dollars in gold, but by the 1920's it was mostly played out.[81]

Livengood grew to a town of several hundred people. But despite the wealth of the gold remaining in the ground, when the government banned gold mining during World War II and froze gold prices at $35 an ounce, Livengood became a ghost town.

"Jay wised up first and sold out." Rich Geraghty recalls, "Ted married a woman named Harriet (Harriet M. McCauley) and kept mining." What's left of their first cabin still remains on the

---

[80] LIVENGOOD The Last Stampede, Audry Parker, Hats Off Books, Tuscon, Arizona
[81] Alaska Sportsman Magazine, Ed Ferrell, October 1967

Geraghty claim. Ted eventually leased the claims and retired to travel with his wife on the royalties.

In 1915 after Teddy and Jay made their big strike at Livengood, Jay returned to Sandusky. Jay and Olive were living in Marion, Ohio in 1910 with their youngest daughter, Ruth. Jay was working as a machinist on a steam dredge.[82]   In 1918 Jay's second daughter Gladys Jayne was born. In 1919 Jay returned to Alaska for a six-month junket to "sell out my claims and prospect". In 1922 Olive's father passed away and by 1926 Olive and Jay have separated and Jay has returned to Fairbanks. Olive and the girls stay at the family home on Warren Street in Sandusky until1941 when they move to Los Angles to live with her brother Charles Doerflinger who is working for the railroad.

Neil Davis included a chapter in his book, 'Battling against Success' which featured Jay and his partner Henry Spraul in a poignant description of the way Jay lived his final years. Jay suffered from heart trouble, and Henry, had been severely crippled in a mining accident. They lived outside of Fairbanks on Piledriver Slough cutting firewood to earn a meager living. For all practical purposes they were dead broke most of the time. They had a timber permit to cut trees behind Mike Bedoff's place on trails they cut through the trees that could only be driven on in the winter when they were frozen. They both cut four-foot cords as opposed to the sixteen-foot cords that were standard for most woodcutters, because Jay was too old and weak to handle the longer wood and Henry was so badly crippled. Henry used two chest high canes to get around. Both men lived year around in separate eight by ten foot, double walled, canvas tents. Each tent had a dirt floor and was

_____

[82] United States census, 1910

equipped with a Yukon stove for cooking and heat. Both tents were modified with a makeshift swing door rather than the usual flap for entry and although there were no windows the thin canvas let in plenty of light. Theirs was a strange partnership because they never worked together but each had his own cutting area and worked alone. Their tents were only about ten feet apart, but communication was sparse. Sometimes they did not talk to each other for weeks at a time. Jay and Henry did not cut very much wood in a year's time, probably about fifty to seventy-five cords apiece. They received seven to ten dollars a cord for their labors, just enough to buy food, candles, files and saw blades. They lived a very frugal existence.

Twice a year Jay and Henry would go into Fairbanks for supplies and mail. Neil describes preparations for the trip as dressing up in their "Alaska Tuxedos" which were a matched wool twill set of pants and jacket with a large game pocket across the back. These outfits were manufactured by the C.C. Filson Co of Seattle and came in green or grey Jay wore gray, Henry green. Their working clothes were identical except that, in the summer when the mosquitoes swarmed the lowlands, Henry soaked his in oil of citronella to repel the ravenous pests.

Neil and his parents tried to anticipate when these trips to town would occur and just and arrange to just 'happen' to come by with their pickup truck to conveniently offer a ride. Their pride would not allow Jay and Henry to accept charity.

The winter before Jay died was very cold with the thermometer registering fifty below for six weeks and sometimes below minus seventy. A month into the cold spell, Jay got sick with dysentery and could not get out of his sleeping bag. One night he stoked his fire so hot that a spark fell on the top of his tent and burned a three by four-foot hole next to the chimney. Henry located in his tent ten feet away was unaware of what had happened because Jay did not call out. He lay there for two weeks until the cold snap broke and his illness was mostly over. He was very weak and needed a new sleeping bag for which Neil's father made a special trip into town.

Jay never fully recovered from that incident. Several months later Jay collapsed and died on the Post Office steps in Fairbanks while visiting with another old timer. He was 72 years of age.[83]

Jay is buried in the Pioneer section of the Birch Hill Cemetery in Fairbanks. He lies at rest next to his old prospecting partner Teddy Hudson and Ted's wife Harriet. Jay's wife Olive passed away in 1964 at age 84 and is interred at a North Hollywood California Cemetery in Los Angeles County.

Photo from FindAGrave.com

---

[83] Battling Against Success, Neil Davis, McRoy & Blackburn, Ester, Alaska

Jay Livengood- 1938

Ross Livengood- 1874-1958

Ross Campbell Livengood was 23 years old in 1897 when the Seattle newspapers announced that gold had been discovered in the Klondike regions of Alaska. At that time Ross was living with his parents, Urban and Gertrude Livengood and his four brothers on their prairie farm four miles west of Milan, Ohio near the community of Enterprise.

At the completion of his contract with the ACM Co. Ross planned to return home with the main party. But circumstances, as they often do, changed those plans. As the party made their way down the Yukon River from Eagle to St. Michaels, where they intended to board a steamer for Seattle, an accident caused Ross to be left behind (Appendix E).

It was pitch dark when Ross heard a voice calling for help on the riverboats upper deck. Rushing up the stairs to give aid to the caller Ross fell through an open hatch into the boat's cargo hold. Hitting his head in the fall he was knocked unconscious, suffering a concussion and a broken leg. Ross had carried two pokes of gold which were tied to his belt under his coat. When he regained consciousness, he was in a hospital at St. Michaels; his gold was gone. The boat's Captain had taken Ross to the hospital where he was laid up for several weeks. The rest of the party continued on except for Frank Adelman, who stayed behind to help Ross until he was out of the hospital. Frank left for home when Ross was well enough to get along by himself.

Finding himself alone and broke in St Michaels, he was determined not to go home empty handed. Ross decided to make one more try for the riches that had brought him to Alaska and went to Nome, where the newest stampede was in progress. This meant he would stay on for another winter in Alaska. The 1900 census finds Ross near Bluff City, Alaska in a tent camp, with his new partner, Ray, panning for gold. Ross finally left Alaska for home in July of 1900.

Ross married Gertrude Stein in 1903. Their daughter Marjorie was born in 1904 and son Urban was born in 1909. Gertrude died in 1951.

Ross lived alone in a cottage at Rye Beach for several years before he died. As he got older, he began to experience heart troubles. His self-prescribed medication for the condition was to set out a shot glass of whiskey on his bed stand before he went to bed each night. He would drink it the first thing each morning before he arose, saying it was to get his heart started. Ross died in his sleep on December 12, 1958. The shot glass of whiskey was found untouched on his bed stand that morning.

Photo from FindAGrave.com

Ross Livengood- 1954

'Nothing will come of him, the stampeder.

He is a whorl in the wind, a brother to the fog.

At the scene of his activity no memory of him will remain.

The gravel he thawed and sifted will freeze again...

The snow will cover his trail, and all will be as before.

-Ambrose Bierce

Appendices

Appendix A.

THE KLONDIKERS SONG

Alaska Co-operative Mining Company,
From Sandusky City we came
And we're going to the city of Dawson'
A'fore we go home again.
There's 20 boys in our company'
All healthy, good and strong'
And to haul our outfit along with us,
We've got two oxen along.

We stopped in the city of Seattle'
Down on seventh street.
We rented an empty store there
To fill our outfit up complete.
Our captain and the advisory board
Kept fetchin' the supplies all in__
We boxed em up, and sleighs all made
And now we're ready to start again.

Cap Snevely is the business man,
He proves to us each day;
That our money is used with care
And that nothing is thrown away.
Our supplies are the best in the market,
Our outfit's good all through;
So we all give him the credit,
And the advisory board too.

We've got guns and ammunition,
And we've got Klondike Dell---
And how many polar bear we'll get
It'll be mighty hard to tell.
And we've got Jim our noble cook,
Who'll be with us everywhere
And Klondike Dell will see
That we have plenty of polar bear.

Then we've got our judge from Dayton,
That left his girl behind___
And is going up to Dawson,
A looking for a mine.
And Perry the barber, he's all right,
When we get ready to stop;
While the judge is looking for a mine
The barber will run the shop.

All you folks that ain't in our camp,
That happens to read our song___
You'd split your sides a laughen'
If you were only just along.
Day and night is all the same;
We just have lots of fun___
It would take ten pounds of paper
To tell you all that's done.

Now there is Charlie Koegle,
Lord how he grinds his teeth.
And there is baby Miller,
It's really my belief___
He can beat any man I ever saw
In my whole life before
That weighs 250 pounds,
When he begins to snore.

There's Addleman, the bull puncher,
So good-natured and long___
And there is Livengood, his partner,
So good-natured and strong.
They are the boys that drive the oxen
Bring the outfit up behind,
While the rest of us is goin' ahead
A looking for a mine.

There is Huntington the bookkeeper,
Keeps the books and carries the keys
Correspondent for the newspaper,
Puts in everything he sees'
He does a great deal of sleepin'
And more of laying around,
And figures up the boys accounts
When they get back from town.

There's Charlie Smith our sailor,
He can splice a rope complete___
He's the greatest, cleverest sailor,
You'll ever chance to meet.
He's the same good-natured sailor,
No matter where he be;
He's Charlie Smith the sailor,
On either land or sea.

Now there are Theim and Fetel,
You bet they are the boys___
You never think about your home,
They are makin' such a noise.
They keep the thing a goin',
You bet you everywhere___
We couldn't do without' em
To drive away dull care.

Now there are Cowan and Meinzer,
By Jove they can't be beat,
For building cabins and making tools,
By Jove they are complete.
And there's old Stewart Widman,
Who buys a bone for meat,
And there is Granddad Gleckner,
Who can make a brick complete.

Ross Livengood, our bike rider,
Has left his wheel behind___
He thought it wouldn't be the thing,
These rugged hills to climb.
But then he'll have another
When we get home again,
Out o' those bags of gold dust,
He going to bring home with him.

Now there is Pat McCrystal,
He don't have much to say,
And Zurcher, the piano maker,
He's laid his trade away.
They are both going up to Dawson,
To see what they can find,
They say they'll never work again
If they just hit a mine.

On the barque Theobold,
It's the ship we'll take to go___
The tug Resolute, will tow her,
She's a safe ship we all know,
She's eighteen hundred tonnage,
A tried ship through and through,
She's got a good commander
And first class sailors too.

We've 30 tons of first class freight,
One outfit mentioned through.
We'll soon be up to Dawson now
To see what we can do.
If you were just along with us,
You bet it would be nice
To see our miners outfit
A slidin' along on ice.
We'll prospect all the gulches,
As we go along the line,
And keep our eyes wide open
To see what we can find.
For we know that in that country,
There is plenty to be found___
We are just going there after it,
And to have it we are bound.

Verses by N.P. Sams [84]

---

[84] The Klondikers Song, Verses by N.P. Sams, *Norwalk Daily Reflector*, 10 February, 1899

Appendix B.

FINANCIAL REPORT
Of The Alaska Co-Operative Mining Company

The board of directors of the Alaska Co-Operative Mining company has issued a financial statement to their stockholders, which gives a full and complete showing of the company's receipts and expenditures to date and completely exonerate Manager Snevely from the charges and insinuations of crookedness in handling the company's funds. The Register will have some further matter to give the public in a day or two, in which many intensely pertinent and interesting facts are given bearing upon the troubles in the camp, and which will let in a flood of light on the whole matter. The director's financial report, it will be observed, is signed by H.C. Huntington and John McCrystal who were appointed an advisory board at the recent stormy meeting of the stockholders.

The financial report is as follows:

Cash receipts- 1,255 shares of capital stock sold at $10/share	$12,550.00
Interest collected on the Sanderson note	$18.00
TOTAL	**$12,568.00**
Cash and letters of credit returned by Snevely	$2,087.78
One duplicate letter of credit now in the mail, which will either be received by men in the field or returned to the treasury	$500.00
TOTAL	**$2,587.78**
GRAND TOTAL	**$15,155.78**

CASH PAID OUT	
Feb. 3, 1898, by cash and expense for incorporation	$25.00
Feb. 5, 1898, by sundry expenses paid J.E. Snevely for 6 months work, railroad fare, and hotel bills of organizing the company	$500.00
Feb. 5, 1898, by paid J.C. Scheufler 18 months salary at $5 per month	$90.00
Feb. 7, 1898, by 20 railroad tickets to Seattle at $35.37 each	$707.40
Feb. 7, 1898, by J.E. Snevely, cash and drafts	$4,500.00
Feb. 7, 1898, by bolls paid in Sandusky	$894.60
Feb. 17, 1898, by J.E. Snevely, agent, letters of credit sent to Seattle	$2,000.00
April 22, 1898, to J.E. Snevely, agent, letters of credit sent to Dawson	$500.00
July 5, 1898, to J.E. Snevely, agent, letters of credit and draft sent to Circle City	$2,000.00
Jan. 17, 1899, to J.E. Snevely, to C.M. Koegle, two drafts at $500.00	$1,000.00
Jan. 31, 1899, to sundry expenses paid to J.E. Snevely for 12 months salary, paid wife	$600.00
TOTAL	**$12,817.00**
CASH BALANCE ON HAND	**$2,338.78**

The board of directors, together with the advisory board composed of H.C. Huntington and John McCrystal have examined the financial report of J.E. Snevely and find from his account that he has received money sent him from Sandusky by the board of directors, various collections and rebates of customs, a sum amounting to $9,893.87; that he has expended the sum of $7,306.09, and has returned to the company cash and letters of credit amounting to $2,087.78, which, together with one unused letter of credit for $500, now with the men in the field or in the mails, will balance his cash account.

This account is approved subject to revision or correction upon procuring bills and vouchers that have been left in camp, or that will be duplicated from the purchasers, if required. So far as we are able to pass upon his account, we see nothing that is not legitimate and proper. His account is on file subject to inspection of the stockholders.

This is only a report showing the financial condition of the corporation, and all other questions and complaints raised by the men in the field are not included or passed upon in this report and are left open for further investigation.

A.E. Merrill, J.C. Scheufler, F.L. Felch, J.C. Parsons, C.L. Wagner, John. C. McCrystal, H.C. Huntington[85]

---

[85] FINANCIAL REPORT, *Norwalk Daily Reflector,* 10 February 1899

Appendix C.

Map of Eagle City Alaska

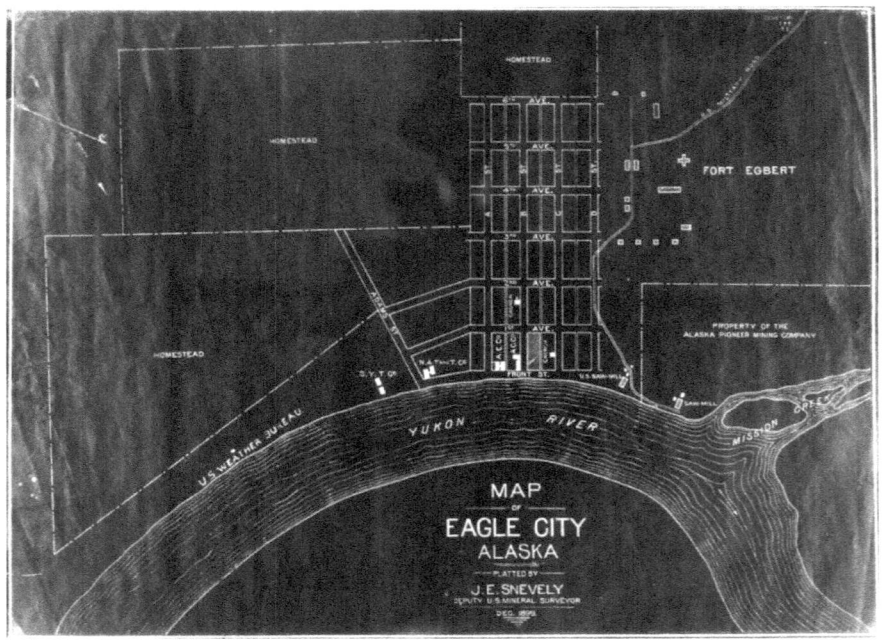

Map of Eagle City, Alaska by J.E. Snevely, Deputy U.S. Mineral
Surveyor, December 1899[86]

---

[86] Map of Eagle City, Alaska, The Elmer Rasmuson Library, University of
Alaska, Fairbanks

Appendix D.

Signed deed to Alaska Cooperative Mining Company

Deed, Cont.   81

... in ... care ... ...
... town, Beginning at a point sixty (60) feet
from the left bank (descending) of the Yukon River at
ordinary high water mark about four thousand
two hundred (4,200) feet up stream from the mouth
of Mission Creek, near Eagle City Alaska, thence
southerly on a line S, 23° W. 510 feet thence easterly
on a line E. 23° S, thirteen hundred twenty feet (1320 ft)
thence northerly on a line N. 23° E. 664 feet to a point
... feet from the said left bank of the said Yukon
River at ordinary high water mark, thence west-
ly along said river bank 60 feet therefrom
and parallel thereto to a point of beginning,
comprising about fifteen acres, and on which is
erected the large log house of said parties of the
first part. To have and to hold the same whith
all and singular the tenements hereditaments and
appurtenances thereunto belonging or in any
wise appertaining. In witness whereof said parties
of the first part have hereunto set their hands
and seals the day and year first above
written. The Alaska Cooperation Mining Co
Charles W. Koegley   L S
J. K. Sanderson   L S
W. J. Dyeo   L S

Recorded
Mch 9. 1899

Geo Miller
Wm Cowen
Wm Settle
Patrick McCrystie
H.R. Huntington
Wm Thiene
Frank Adelman
Ross. C. Livengood
J. Livengood
J. A. Shay
Perry Hatchins
H. U. Zurcher
Sylvester Widman
George Gieckler
Chas Smith
Abram Menzie

Witness
J.T. Hobber
J. Chapman

District of Alaska } ss
Eagle City

On this 9th day
of March 1899. before me a notary Public
in and for said District of Alaska
Personally appeared the within named

Appendix E.

Post card from Jay Livengood to Gertrude Livengood